DYNAMICS OF ECONOMIC LIFE IN RURAL INDIA

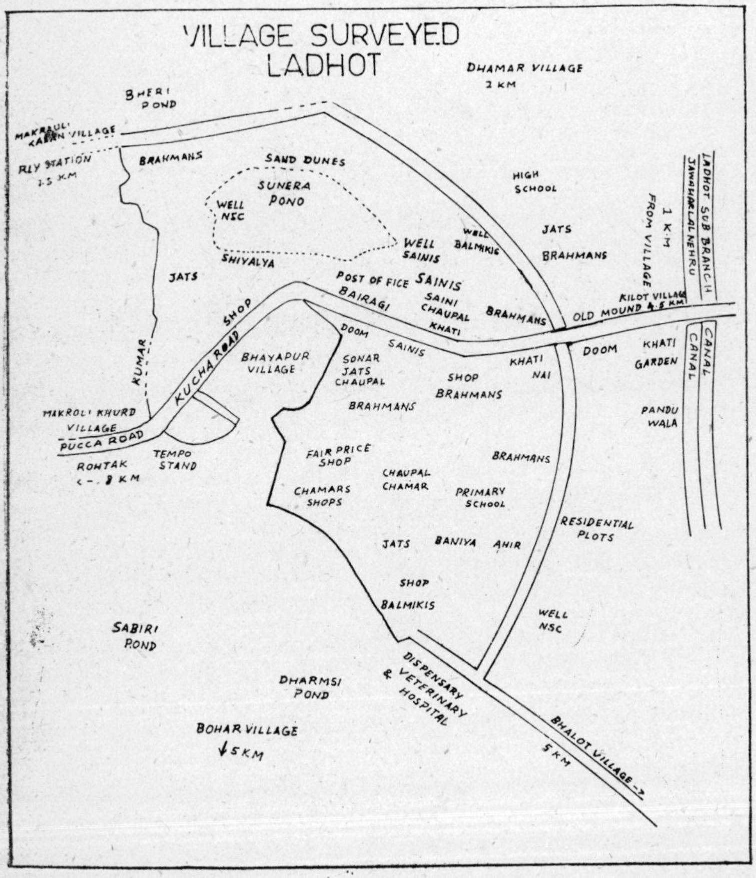
VILLAGE SURVEYED
LADHOT
DHAMAR VILLAGE
2 KM
BHERI
POND
MAKRAULI KALAN VILLAGE
RLY STATION
BRAHMANS
SAND DUNES
SUNERA
POND
WELL
NSC
HIGH
SCHOOL
LADHOT SUB BRANCH
JAWAHARLAL NEHRU
1 KM
FROM VILLAGE
JATS
WELL
BALMIKIS
WELL
SAINIS
BRAHMANS
SHIYALYA
JATS
POST OF FICE
SAINIS
BAIRAGI
SAINI
CHAUPAL
KHATI
KILOT VILLAGE
OLD MOUND 4.5 KM
BRAHMANS
SHOP
DOOM
SAINIS
DOOM
KHATI
GARDEN
CANAL
CANAL
KHATI
NAI
BHAYAPUR
VILLAGE
SONAR
JATS
CHAUPAL
SHOP
BRAHMANS
KUMAR
KUCHA ROAD
BRAHMANS
PANDU
WALA
MAKROLI KHURD
VILLAGE
PUCCA ROAD
TEMPO
STAND
FAIR PRICE
SHOP
BRAHMANS
ROHTAK
CHAUPAL
CHAMAR
CHAMARS
SHOPS
PRIMARY
SCHOOL
RESIDENTIAL
PLOTS
JATS
BANIYA
AHIR
SHOP
BALMIKIS
WELL
NSC
SABIRI
POND
DISPENSARY
& VETERINARY
HOSPITAL
DHARMSI
POND
BOHAR VILLAGE
5 KM
BHALOT VILLAGE
5 KM

DYNAMICS OF ECONOMIC LIFE IN RURAL INDIA

Dr. L.N. Dahiya

Foreword by

Dr. Har Swarup Singh
Lt Governor, Pondicherry

GIAN

GIAN PUBLISHING HOUSE

NEW DELHI - 110002

GIAN PUBLISHING HOUSE
4-C Ansari Road, Daryaganj
New Delhi-110002

ISBN 81—212—0391—0

PRINTED IN INDIA

Published by Mrs. Gayatri Garg for Gian Publishing House,
New Delhi 110002.
Printed at Godwall Printers, Delhi

Dedicated to
the memory of my grand-parents
Shri Jodha Ram and Smt. Sawrup Rani
with reverence and affection

Foreword

Dr. L.N. Dahiya has successfully endeavoured to project a comprehensive picture of the socio-economic conditions of the people living in the village of Ladhot situated in Rohtak District of Haryana. His analysis is based on a detailed survey of all the 371 households in the village. The author's rural background and personal experience have added sharpness to his observations. The book with its six chapters presents an analytical description of all factors concerned directly or indirectly with the village economy. The author has imparted strength to his conclusions by drawing from a wide range of statistical data included profusely in all Chapters. The findings of the survey report point to the changing face of the rural life, thanks to the impact of various rural development programmes. Such programmes. despite their shortcomings, have left the mark on the village folk and life pattern. For instance, farming in the village has become more productive through the use of fertilizers, improved implements and tractorization, tubewell irrigation, adoption of HYV seeds, better roads and electricity. The village life has also become more comfortable due to better communication, medical and other facilities. It is discovered that most of the people are not lost in blind traditions ; they are now more amenable to socio-economic changes. People are also becoming politically aware and technologically receptive.

At the same time, the author has spotlighted the areas of

failure and shortfalls in achievement. He has brought into focus the deficiencies in educational infrastructure of the village as also the regressive impact of unemployment, rural indebtedness, castc panchayat system, malnutrition and such other economic and social ills on the life-style of the villagers.

Dr. Dahiya has sketched the village in reference to its economy, social life, aspirations, frustration and handicaps of the people in simple terms. The book is an eye opener not only for villagers, it is sufficiently oriented to promote realistic thinking on the part of those who plan for the villages. Actual involvement of common man in the village in the process of planning is essential for any meaningful exercise. Dr. Dahiya is, however, optimistic and feels strongly that poverty and other problems are uot impossible to eradicate povided there is political will and commitment to realistic policies. This underlines the need for integrating the people-led process of planning at the micro-level and coordinating it with initiatives at higher levels.

Thus, the solution to the basic problems of rural India lies in the strategy of our economic planning. The author's endeavour deserves encouragement, as we do not have the village-wise basic data pertaining to the different aspects of socio-economic life of the people. Such a scientific and analytical study of each and every village is a pre-requisite for initiating the process of planning at the grassroots level. I am sure that Dr. Dahiya's publication containing a positive analysis of the complexities of the changing economic and social life of the people in the small village of Ladhot will be a very useful guide in this direction.

Raj Nivas
Pondicherry

HAR SWARUP SINGH
LIEUTENANT GOVERNOR

Preface

Interest in rural problems is growing rapidly in India. Ever since independence there has been an insistent demand for integrated rural development in the country. It was realized that it is only the socio-economic transformation at village level that would really contribute to positive change in India. Many attempts have been made by the governments both at the centre and state levels to orient rural economy to new heights of development and to promote social justice through various policy, programmes and strategies.

However, there is ample evidence to show that despite the efforts made through various programmes, an ordinary villager has remained the victim of circumstances and never the master. Poverty, hunger, unemployment and other social taboos still haunt the spectre of the Indian rural economy. Even a shift from a macro level planning to district and block level planning has not made a significant dent in the colossal problem of unemployment and poverty of the rural masses. Perhaps, this is mainly because of lack of political will, inept and inefficient administration, defective planning and wrong priorities.

This study presents, through its six chapters, some of the important socio-economic aspects of the village named Ladhot. The village eight kms. from Rohtak city is covered by Community Development Block and falls in district Rohtak, Haryana. In order to know the village a host of factors like agriculture, rural assets, occupational structure, unemployment, indices of poverty, savings and borrowings, communication, education, nutrition and health and several other aspects have been considered. The detailed analysis, however, has been kept limited to those factors only which were made challenging and which helped us most to understand the village under study.

The field work in connection with the survey of the village was undertaken by a field investigator Mrs. Yaswanti, during the months of April-September 1985. She covered all the 371 households in the village. Understandably, in a study like this, where all the aspects of the village are to be studied, any amount of work would appear to the wanting in some resspect or the other while drafting the report. This took me to the village several times for filling such gaps which existed in the data. Not only this, I personally collected secondary data also and tapped all the relevant sources. The mass of primary and secondary data so collected was tabulated by Mr. Durga Dutt who worked as tabulator-cum-computer for the project. The writing of the report, being a lengthy procedure, took me more than two years to complete.

It is pertinent to mention that this report is an outcome of the research project sanctioned to me by the M.D. University, Rohtak, in February 1985. I owe an immense debt of gratitude to the university for financial support to meet the varied types of expenses incurred on the project. I owe humble gratitude to Dr. D.S. Dalal for thoroughly reading the manuscript and contributing valuable suggestions. I am deeply indebted to Dr. Har Swarup Singh for writing the Foreword. I am also grateful to Dr. M.G. Gandhi, Dr. S. Kaushil and Dr. R.P. Hooda for their interest in the project. I am grateful to my students namely Dr. S.D. Vashistha Dr. Daharam Sukh, Roshan Lal, Rajkumar, Satish Bansal, Kuldeep Singh Malik and Mohinder who assisted me in a more general way, in preparing this work.

My thanks are also due to government officials at the district and village level, particularly, Rattan Lal, the village Patwari, who unhesitatingly extended the co-operation during the field survey and made available ungrudgingly all the village records. I am also indebted to the residents of the village who co-operated with us with the best of courtesy. They remained hospitable and generous despite the irksome demands made by us in asking even the sensitive and personal information. I owe special thanks to Mr. Jawala Ram, a grand old man of the village (now not living) who could narrate vividly the important village events spanning over a century. Lastly, to my wife, Shakuntla, and children, Seema, Kusum and Sujata, I owe thanks that cannot be adequately expressed. I would like to thank Mr. B.P. Garg for taking pains in getting the book through the press with his personal care.

I hope that the material presented in the report will be useful to all concerned in formulating policy and programmes for the village and all other similar villages. This would also prove provocative for further observation and thought on the subject.

Rohtak
January 1991

L.N. Dahiya

Contents

CHAPTER 1

INTRODUCTION

The Study

Real India lives in its sprawling six lakh villages comprising about 80 per cent of the total population. Necessarily, it is the economic transformation of these villages that can bring about a meaningful change in India's economic development. In other words, the progress and prosperity of our nation depends entirely on how far we are able to improve the economic and social life of the rural masses. In view of the realisation of this fact governments at the centre and in the states have made various attempts, through numerous rural development programmes, to change the face of rural India.

In the wake of such programmes there occurred a lot of research into village communities in India to assess the impact of these programmes on the socio-economic life of the villagers. A review of the relevant literature would reveal that there are now available a plethora of rural studies made from time to time by economists, sociologists and anthropologists both from India and abroad. The beginning of village studies is marked by the appearance of two outstanding works, namely *Village Com-*

munities in the East and West and *Village Communities in India* written by Sir Henry Maine and Badden-Powell respectively. These studies appearing towards the middle of the 19th century, have led much more to the understanding of peasant society in its many fold aspects—evolutionary, historical, political, economic and theoretical. Since 1920, there have been several outstanding community studies in India and abroad which made valuable contribution to the close understanding of village and its life. The period between 1940-56 has been quite significant in India and elsewhere where some more notable works appeared in this field which helped in visualising the emergence of community studies as a special branch of study. Many educational institutions, social scientists, researchers, research organisations, governmental machineries, journals, periodicals etc. evinced great interest in such studies and played very significant role during this period. These agencies have clearly established the need to explore the hitherto neglected peasantry which makes up the bulk of population in the underdeveloped countries including India.

In India, the period after independence witnessed near revolution in the rural studies and several village studies were conducted almost in all the Indian states. Among the notable researches on various aspects of rural life in pre-independence and post-independence periods, the names of the following are worth mentioning : M.L. Darling, Oscar Lewis, W.H. Newell, B.S. Cohen, G.P. Steed, M.N.Srinivas, S.C.Dube, R.K.Mukherjee, I.Karve, A.R.Desai, K.Ishwaran, William H.Wiser, Charlotte Viall Wiser, Tom. G.Kissinger, M.L.Dantwala and Jahir Ahmed. More recently C.J.Bliss and N.H. Stern have completed a rural study and set a new dimension in this direction. They have in their study made a systematic attempt to put the test of the theories of under-development and of the motives and behaviour of rural people in the village of Palanpur, situated in Moradabad district in Uttar Pradesh. The authors while reporting on the village and its institutions reviewed the development models, modified them where they deemed appropriate for policy and for the future growth of the village.

Besides these, a number of research journals continue to maintain progress in the direction and are keeping abreast with the latest development in the field. Research articles are published in these journals specialized in rural economy and its problems. Institutions like UNESCO, Ford Foundation, Indian Council of Social Science Research, Planning Commission and Universities give financial support, scholarships and fellowships for undertaking rural projects. It can now be safely said that village studies have become an integral part of modern researches. Through these village studies some vital facts of village life have been revealed covering different geographical and cultural regions of the country. At present there are many more research projects which are in progress under the supervision of highly eminent professors and scholars in universiti and research institutes within and outside the country. And we hope to offer, on the basis of these studies under way, scientific and lasting solutions of multifarious problems of rural life from growing poverty to appalling indebtedness of the villages, with a view to ensuring them a better future in the years to come.

Today, villages in Haryana are in the process of change and transformation mainly due to the introduction of various rural developmental programmes. Moreover, the advent of science and technology has greatly contributed to accelerate the process and to bring about immense changes in several important aspects of the village. The important aspects of village life which are in a process of change are the economic system, system of communication, its rituals and taboos. Our main concern in the study, no doubt, is an economic one, but we shall also analyse briefly social aspects and also the affiliation of the village of external influences. The study would highlight the factors responsible for change, whether gradual or sudden, major or minor, in the structure and organisation of the village. In fact, there are several important issues and questions which deserve consideration in the scientific and systematic study of an Indian village. Therefore, an attempt is made here to provide answers to these unsdetled questions.

Mostly our analysis, based on facts, will run in terms of

castes and their groups. Each caste has its own cultural heritage and in that sense more often acts independently of other castes. While caste prescription finds expression in the behaviour of the members, conformity to prevailing usages, norms and values in a large measure accounts for the differences among villages. Caste, which is rooted in the religion and has been reared by the socio-economic forces and recognised by the political structure still occupies a pivotal place in the village life.

While making selection of the village for the purpose of this study we were not looking for the village as representative as there is no such thing as the representative village. But we surely wanted to select a village large enough to encompass a certain amount of variety but not too large to permit a detailed study of the entire population. We wanted the village to be accessible from Rohtak but at the the same time not so close to the city. We also wanted to select a village representing sufficient number of castes, occupation diversity and population. Another point of consideration was that the village should also not be notably an oddity. Ladhot village met all these criteria suitably and hence the selection. Ladhot is one of the 438 inhabited villages of Rohtak district which is one of the 14 districts of Haryana state. Confining the study to a single village has several attractions. It allowed, through the people in the village, a close involvement with the households which formed the village and with the village institutions. It could be possible to have a great insight into the problem of all the 371 households in the village.

The Collection of the Data

To conduct such a study we required primary as well as secondary data. Since there existed not any kind of enquiry of this village before so we had to collect information from the scratch with great efforts. Before beginning the collection of primary data from the households general information of the village was obtained from the following different sources and agencies.

(i) District Statistical Office,
(ii) District Library,
(iii) Block Development Office,
(iv) Land Development Bank,
(v) District Gazetteer,
(vi) Revenue Records of the Patwari,
(vii) Schools' Records, and
(viii) Gram Panchayat Records.

The above sources provided some information and details, enabling us to have a general picture of the village under study. The records were carefully studied for demographic, economic and certain social statistics. But the data obtained through these above mentioned sources was scanty not sufficient to construct a coherent picture of the village. Therefore, the data were made available through field work. The actual field work for the project commenced in April 1985 which continued for a total period of six months. The investigator who assisted the project in the matter of data collection was supervised closely by me. The data was collected by a door-to-door survey method of all the 371 households in the village. The most commonly used methods of schedule and questionnaire along with the techniques of interview were employed for the purpose. A questionnaire was framed to cover various items that formed the part of economic and social structure in the village. Pre-testing of the questionnaire was done to see if it worked well, and on the basis of observations, necessary changes were made in it. It was later got printed from the University Press and administered personally by the field workers in a face-to-face interview with the respondents. Counter-questions were made where found necessary and observations noted in the empty space provided in the questionnaire for the purpose. Information was also collected, however, in a number of additional ways. Investigator and myself often had lengthy discussions with the households to extract some personal and sensitive information. To the extent possible, the head of the household was contacted for family information.

The collection of data regarding different aspects of village life required different approaches. Some, such as the family data, were collected at one go whilst the labour data, for example, required regular monitoring. This demanded alertness, cross-checking, and continual observation of what was going on. We always obtained information both from the landlord and from the tenant, and often from friends and known. In addition to the formal questions we conversed regularly with the villagers, observed day-to-day happenings, and took notes of what we learnt. Some embarrassing questions on family planning and indebtedness were asked in the end mostly from the neighbours and financial institutions. As pointed out, all our questionnaires contained space for notes and remarks on peculiarities and points of special interest concerning villagers. This non-systematic information proved to be valuable and it was drawn on frequently in the text. The interview was conducted in Haryanvi, the spoken language of the respondents.

It may be pointed out that to start with people were hesitant to give information. But this attitude was short lived. As the investigator belonged to this village, she gradually overcame the suspicions of the village people regarding the survey. It was explained to them that the survey is meant for their well-being. They on being assured thus cooperated. Most of the villagers did not shrink even at the outset from revealing to us. Whenever I visited the village to supervise the survey and to get additional information from the village elders and others, the people met me with kindness and generosity. People were quite hospitable and they welcomed my visits. Because of the factors explained above and the mutual trust the survey went off smoothly and authoritative information could be collected without much difficulty.

Plan of the Study

The study has been divided into 6 Chapters including the one Introduction. Chapter 2 describes the village, its history, and its institutions. Chapter 3 deals with the economic structure of the village. It also provides a brief review of certain issues which commonly occur in discussions of Indian agriculture and allied activities on which we could comment in the light of our experience in the village. Chapter 4 is concerned mainly with the social and cultural life, power authority and influence in the village. Chapter 5 examines the impact of developmental programmes on the village life and also the responses of the people to these programmes. The 6th and the final chapter contains a brief summary and broad conclusions of the study. Two appendices have been added : appendix 'A' contains the questionnaire and appendix 'B' gives the glossary of the local terms employed in the text.

CHAPTER 2

THE VILLAGE

This Chapter presents a comprehensive description of the village named Ladhot in origin, location, residential arrangement, population, institutions and caste structure. Essentially, the purpose of this chapter is to furnish the necessary background of the village and to premise the basic reference material for subsequent chapters.

Origin of Village

Nothing is available on record as how and when the village 'Ladhot' came to be first inhabited. There is no mention about it in the gazetteer of Rohtak district. However, villagers are able to narrate several stories about the origin and existence of the village. One guess is that the village is quite antique and existed even during the Mahabharata time. They identify the village with a place where Pandavas lived in their exile. According to the legend the name of a field 'Panduwala' in the village is derived from nothing else but the Pandavas. The belief is that Hastinapur, the capital city of the Pandavas, was deserted by them during their period of exile and they once lived in and around this village. The popular folk verse which has been in currency since time immemorial is :

"Hastinapur Sunni Pari,
Ladhot Mein Do Sankh Baje."

(Hastinapur lies deserted. But in Ladhot were blows of two conch shells).

The belief is that there used to be two sounds of conch blowing in the village—one by a contemporary saint who lived in the village and the other by Pandavas. If this identification is believed then the village is of least two thousand and five hundred years old. There stands an old mound near the village where once this ancient village of Ladhot was inhabited. The excavation of the mound is expected to shed some more light on the origin and hoary past of the village. Recently, some excavation work was reported to be carried out which yielded some valuable terracotta reinforcing the belief of its ancient existence.

This account lends credence to the view that Ladhot is an ancient village with a rich cultural past. Though it is very difficult to say exactly when it was founded but it seems almost certain that it is an old village. The origin of 'Deswal' a sub-caste among Jats is stated to be from this village. 'Deswals' scattered and settled themselves in Haryana and the adjoining state of Uttar Pradesh from this village and now they have many villages where this caste dominates. In Haryana alone there are about 25 such villages. Whenever, caste panchayat is held to consider some common social problem faced by the community then all Deswal villages look to Ladhot for advice and final decision. Thus, the Deswals of this village are held in high esteem by all other Deswals settled in Haryana, Uttar Pradesh and elsewhere. The entire village speaks Haryanvi and Hindi.

Location

The village Ladhot is situated at 28°19' and 29°4' north latitude and 76°13' and 76°58' east longitude in north eastern corner of Rohtak city in Haryana state. It is about 8 kilometres from the district headquarters of Rohtak and is connected with all season metalled road. It is situated on an undulating surface at sufficient elevation. The village Makroli Kalan lies on its west at a distance of one and a half-kilometre, Kiloi to its east about four and a half kilometers and to the south at the same distance stand the village of Bohar. The village Bhayapur which is just adjacent to Ladhot, is also on its south. To its north two kilometres away is village Dhamar. The villages surrounding Ladhot are more or less the size of Ladhot excepting village Kiloi which is much bigger in area and population.

The village is covered by the Community Development Block, Rohtak. The native means of transport for personal and commercial purposes are tractors, bicycles and scooters. The canal 'The Bhalot Sub-Branch' which irrigates lands of this village flows on its eastern border about one kilometre away. Another canal 'The Jawahar Lal Nehru Canal' (JLNC) also runs parallel to 'The Bhalot Sub-Branch'. People also sink tubewells and irrigate their fields. Land though fertile is also affected by salinity and water-logging. The soil is good and quite suitable for raising a variety of agricultural crops. The soil is of two types namely, sandy and sandy-loam. The sandy soil is suitable for jowar, bajra and gram crops while sandy-loam is fit for paddy, wheat and sugarcane. Ground water is available at depth of about 12 feet. Here, wheat and sugarcane are the two main crops. Sugarcane is preferred because of the proximity of the sugar factory at Rohtak. The total geographical area of the village is 671 hectares.

Climate

The climate is generally conducive for the physical health of the people. It is characterised by dry hot summer followed by a spell of rainy season and then cold and pleasant winter. The Table 2.1 indicate the climatic conditions monthwise.

The summer season starts from April and lasts till June. June is the hottest month of the year when the temperature tends to exceed 45°C. The relief from the excessively dry and oppressive heat begins in July after the onset of mon-

TABLE 2.1

Monthly Variation in the Temperature and Rainfall

Month	Temperature °C			Rainfall (Millimetres)
	Maximum	Minimum	Mean	Average 79-83
January	25.1	2.5	13.6	18.1
February	27.4	3.4	16.1	17.7
March	33.9	10.1	21.5	27.9
April	41.2	12.6	25.1	20.3
May	43.3	20.1	39.9	24.2
June	45.3	21.5	32.5	51.0
July	39.5	22.9	31.6	196.0
August	41.0	23.1	31.0	119.9
September	36.8	19.0	28.6	39.8
October	37.3	13.9	25.7	11.3
November	33.0	7.9	20.7	10.9
December	28.5	3.2	15.9	7.4

Source : *Statistical Abstract Haryana 1984-85* issued by E.S.O Haryana, Chandigarh.

Note : Figures for temperature relate to 1984 for Hissar Zone which includes Rohtak. Maximum and minimum temperature at any point of time in a month.

Mean = 1/2 (mean daily maximum plus mean daily minimum temperature during the month)

soon. The rainy season comes to an end by the end of September. The prospects of good crops, to a greater extent, depend on the timely and adequate rainfall and failure of it means bad agricultural conditions. The winter season starts in November and lasts till mid-March. January is the coldest month with the average maximum daily temperature of 25.1°C and the minimum 2.5°C. During cold wave, temperature goes down near to the freezing point when it affects the animals and crops alike.

Residential Arrangement

The residential arrangement is quite peculiar in the village. The village appears to be divided into caste quarters. But it is not easy to determine the boundaries of these blocks without some investigation. Entering the village from the western side and along the road, one finds that the first cluster of houses belongs to the Kumhar community. The number of castes in the village which count as many as 15 occupy more or less distinct and separate localities. The village has people belonging to two religions—Hindu and Muslim. The Muslim group comprising only 13 Doom families is a small group and lives in a separate locality on the eastern edge of the village. The Jats, the largest group of households, is found dispersed throughout the village. The Sainis, the next predominant caste in number, are found in the north-east of the village. It is obvious from the village map that certain specific castes with some families are mostly huddled together at one place. Most of the families of Brahmins find themselves in the heart of the village. Chamar and Balmiki, these two Scheduled Castes, are mostly located on the southern periphery of the village but not segregated completely from the main locality. These are in separate cluster but are closely linked together. Khatis are seen clustered at three places. After investigating the residential pattern in the village, it becomes clear that caste hierarchy has influenced village habitation in the past though now losing its rigidity.

Regarding the arrangements of houses, these are built close up against each other and the lanes between them are narrow with many turns, some of them abrupt and also blind.

The lanes are both *pucca* and *kucha*. It is very dark at night, as there is no proper arrangement for street lights though electricity was introduced in the village about 25 years back. Some lanes are dingy full of holes making it very difficult to cross not only during rainy season but even in summer season. The decoration pattern of houses is almost the same without any distinctive fancy patterns on the exterior of the walls. Almost all the houses are pucca excepting 38 kucha houses which belong mostly to the Scheduled Castes. The kucha houses have mud walls and are weather beaten. The houses of the Scheduled Castes are quite modest. Most of the houses are built in old and traditional style. There are also houses in the village which are quite spacious, double storeyed and with an urban architectural touch.

Area and Population

The total area of the village is 671 hectares out of which 590 hectares are under cultivation in the hands of cultivating farmers. About 87 per cent of the cultivated land is under irrigation and only 13 per cent unirrigated. Canal is the main source of irrigation. The major crops of the village are wheat, sugarcane, paddy and bajra. The surplus agricultural produce is usually marketed in Rohtak.

The village population is estimated to be 2372 persons in the survey year 1985. A study of the growth of households and population of the village can be made from Table 2.2.

It may be seen from Table 2.2 that the population of the village grew from 1496 in the year 1961 to 2372 in the year 1985. This gave an absolute increase of 876 persons and a percentage increase of 58.6 during this period. It is quite interesting to compare population figures in different census years. In between 1961 and 1971, the population growth of 26.5 per cent was quite high. But in the subsequent periods the rate of population growth slowed down. In between 1971 and 1981, the rise in population was 17.2 per cent and the increase from 1981 to 1985 was 7.0 per cent. The rapid increase in population in the decade 1961-71 is attributed to the fall in death rate due to the control of malaria and the

TABLE 2.2

Area, Population and Households

Year	Area (Hectares)	Population (Number)	Males		Females		Houses (Number)
			Number	Percentage	Number	Percentage	
1961	671	1496	777	51.9	719	48.1	204
1971	671	1892	967	51.1	925	48.9	251
1981	671	2217	1184	53.4	1033	46.6	306
1985	671	2372	1337	56.4	1035	43.6	371

Source : Census Reports.

absence of any epidemics in the village. Besides, other medical facilities to the village have also helped in bringing down the death rate. The slowing down of the population after 1971 on the other hand, may be due to control of fertility and the launching of family welfare programmes.

In the case of sex ratio, the trend has been in favour of a masculine population. This trend persisted throughout and is evident from the above table 2.2. There is an excess of males over famales. There are now 77 females per 100 males. The ratio has declined over the time period. For instance, there were 93 females per 100 males in 1961. The reasons for this imbalance in sex ratio are numerous. This can be explained, to some extent, due to insufficient attention and care given to girls after birth. Other factors like race, climate, season of gestation may also be accounted for this situation.

It is also evident from the table that like population the number of houses also increased. The number of houses which was 204 in 1961 increased to 371 in 1985 registering an increase of about 82 per cent. Noteworthy, the percentage increase in the number of houses had been larger than the corresponding percentage increase in population. The implication is that many joint families disintegrated into nuclear ones who in turn built up their own independent dwellings, giving spurt in house building activities in the village.

Literacy

The village shows a good spread of literacy among its people. Out of a total of 2372 persons, 37.1 per cent are literates which gives a higher figure than the district literacy rate.

The level of literacy in the village has gone up from 15.2 per cent in 1961 to 23.9 per cent in 1971 and then to 37 per cent in 1981. It may be noticed that literacy is biased in favour of males. In case of female, the percentage of literacy, though on the increase, is still less than 20 per cent. It was mere 3.6 per cent in 1961. Obviously the parents now take more interest in educating their daughters and the idea that educated daughters make them licentious has no ground. Education for the girls is no longer considered superfluous.

TABLE 2.3

Literacy Rate of Village Population

Year	Literate					
	Total		Male		Female	
1961	227	(15.2)	201	(25.9)	26	(3.6)
1971	452	(23.9)	356	(36.8)	96	(10.4)
1981	822	(37.1)	622	(52.5)	200	(19.4)

Note : Figures in parentheses show the percentage literacy to total population.

The rising trend of female literacy in the village confirms this fact. There is however, no adult literacy centre in the village and, therefore, literacy among the people in the age groups 40-60 and above cannot be expected to increase. Another disquieting feature of the village education is that a large number of pupils drop out either at the primary or middle or high stage schooling without completing their courses which results in considerable wastage in education.

Communication

There are several channels of transport and communication like the railway, road, radio, television, newspaper and post-office through which Ladhot is connected with the world outside. The village is linked with district headquarters with a metalled road that was constructed by the Public Works Department, Haryana (PWD) in 1971-72. This is the only road route from the village to reach Rohtak. The route remains open throughout the year and three wheeled scooters ply on the road to transport the passengers to and from the village. A bus of the Haryana Roadways also plied for some time on this route but was abandoned since this route of only 8 kilometres in length did not prove viable operationally. The scooters, tractors and bicycles are the other means of transportation. The nearest Railway station of Makroli Kalan is 3 kilometres away from the village and there are five train timings. However, 'Ekta Express' a fast train from Bhiwani to Kalka introduced a few years back does not stop here. But now-a-days villagers make little use of train facility from this station as they do not find it very convenient. Before the construction of metalled road in the village the railway facility was fairly in use.

The village is linked with surrounding villages either by a cart track or by a narrow foot-track. These tracks are cut across at a number of places by rivulets and water courses. The surrounding villages mentioned earlier are important for the Ladhot people for their social, economic and political connections.

The village also maintains outside communication through

a good number of people who have gone in service and private business and settled in various towns and cities in the country. Therefore, through the operation of village kinship ties and inter-village organization, Ladhot is not starved of information. Besides these sources, the village also gets outside information through radio, newspaper, television and post office.

Market and Shops

The village has no market centre at one set place. Some 10 odd and tiny shops are dispersed throughout the village which cater to the urgent needs of the villagers. The villagers have to go to Rohtak to transact most of the goods and commodities like food-grains, oil-seeds, clothes, ornaments, footwears, all agricultural accessories, furniture, utensils and medicines.

The villagers visit Rohtak market for the purpose of selling surplus agriculture produce and to purchase the items of their requirement. No doubt some of the commodities they acquire from the city market are also available at the village shops but those purchased from Rohtak market are available at lower rates in larger variety and also fresh. When the villagers visit Rohtak occasionally for some work in the courts or district offices, those who can afford purchase articles for the households.

Surprisingly, shops of various kinds at the bus stand or tempo stand generally found in many villages are not seen here. This is owing to the fact that Ladhot is a village which is neither often visited by outsiders nor is a central bus route. There comes up occasionally at the tail end of the road some *kiosk* where tea prepared on a stove is served in china cups and saucers to the customers.

As already reported, there are about 10 shops in the village. The number of shops owned caste-wise are : Punjabi (4), Jats (2), and Baniya, Brahmin, Lohar and Balmiki one each. The shops are usually run in the residential houses and generally front room of the house serves as shop. These shops are not big ones. The major commodities which they sell are vegetables, inferior quality fruit and sweets, salt and some spices and other grocery items and provisions such as kerosene, stationery, washing shop, *bidis*, cigarettes and tobacco. There is only one shop which exclusively deals in cloth though not in ready-made garments. These shop-keepers acquire articles in whole-sale for their shops from the town market and carry these on cycle or scooter daily or on alternate days. All the shopkeepers in the village sell their merchandise on cash, credit and kind. Out of 10 shops in the village, six are owned by the villagers and four by outsiders. Interestingly, all the four outsiders come to the village to run their shops only in day time and return by evening to Rohtak where they have their abodes. There is also a fair price ration shop in the village which provides essential commodities like sugar, rice and kerosene oil. But these items are supplied in limited quantity on some fixed rates and days against the ration cards. The shop is reportedly not functioning well and items generally remain out of stock.

Village Institutions

The village institutions in Ladhot play very significant role in its all-round development. We now describe the village institutions like schools, panchayat, dispensary, post-office, police-station, *chaupals*, temples, wells, ponds and fields and other government departments and village officials.

Schools : There are two schools in the village namely the Government Primary Girls School and Government High School. The primary school for girls came into existence around 1960 and is located in the heart of the village. The primary school is housed in a very simple two room structure without any window in the back wall. And teaching is nearly all in open air. The total area of the school measures 290 square metres only. The number of students receiving education in this school is 199, out of which 38 belonged to Scheduled Castes and the Backward Classes. There are five teachers in all (four male and one female) who with the exception of a lady teacher reside outside the village. There are two other employees working in the school—one waterman and another a sweeper on part-time basis. There are no chairs and other furniture worth the name in the school and the students sit on bare floor in rows without any mat.

Another school, the Government High School in the village was upgraded in the year 1985 and provides education upto 10th class through Hindi medium. The curriculum includes all the main subjects. It may be mentioned that this school was merely a primary school till 1979 when it was upgraded to a middle school and subsequently gave impetus for the establishment of a high school. This was made possible all due to the efforts of the villagers. The elevated status of the school was wholly due to villagers' efforts which amply reflects their understanding of the need for education. There are also plans for further development of the school. The villagers collected funds and constructed the school building entirely from their own resources. The villagers have again raised a tidy sum of Rs. 80,000 for completing the remaining joinery work in the school.

The school provides co-education after sixth class. Significantly, introduction of co-education indicates their acceptance of the new dimensions of modernism. The number of students on rolls in the school in the survey year was 589 of which 491 were boys and 98 girls. About 20 students from Makroli Khurd and nearly 145 from Bhayapur village attend this school. The number of Scheduled Castes and Backward Class students are 78 and 50 respectively. The number of teaching staff is 20 out of which 17 are males and the rest 3 females. There was reported no shortage of teaching staff. Three of the teachers possess post-graduate qualifications. Besides the teaching staff, there is one clerk and one Physical Trained Instructor (PTI). It is sad that the headmaster and all other teachers do not reside in the village. They come daily either from nearby villages or from Rohtak city.

The school building located on one edge of the village is commodious and surroundings are hygienic. The school has 20 rooms and one office and its campus sprawl over two-and-a half hectares of land. But in terms of other essential facilities the school lacks in woefully. There is no separate library in the school and some 250 odd books are lying with a lady incharge. Medical facilities to the students are non-existent. There is no furniture of any kind for the students. Science room was not well equipped and was not impressive at all.

There were only three electric fans in the entire school. No serious efforts are made to organise cultural and other activities for the good of the students and there is no N.C.C. unit in the school. The attendance in both the schools remains quite thin and students just loiter around aimlessly in shabby dresses. The impression is that the teaching in both the schools is not effective although the middle standard examination result was shown as 70.5 per cent in the year 1985-86.

Panchayat : The village Panchayat is an important organ in the development of Ladhot. The Gram Panchayat in the village is elected periodically and is endowed with legal and fiscal powers. It is completely different from the traditional Panchayat. The Panchayat is coming to be recognised as that branch of administration which must eventually take charge of the expanding social and economic services of the village. It has been assigned a vital and strategic role in rural development. The village Panchayat serves as a major link between the villagers and local administration including the police and revenue officers.

The existing village Panchayat was elected in 1982 for five years and is the sixth Panchayat in succession since the inception of Panchayati Raj. The present Panchayat comprises 8 members and is headed by one Deewan Singh, a Jat. Castewise representation of members is : Jats (3 including a lady), Brahmin, (1) Sunar, (1) Chamar, (1) and Balmiki (2). All but the Sarpanch are illiterates. The Sarpanch has received education upto middle standard. There are relatively older and mature people on the Panchayat. It is a welcome feature of the village Panchayat that most of the members are common and ordinary villagers who do not possess much of land and other valuables. For instance, the Sarpanch possesses hardly one hectare of land and does not own amy conspicuous asset. Another distrinct feature of the present Panchayat is that all the members are new and were elected on the Panchayat body for the first time.

The Panchayat has no office of its own and the meetings take place generally in the house of Sarpanch. As indicated earlier, the functions of the statutory Gram Panchayat now-a-days are often related to the decentralization of political powers and decision-making. The Gram Panchayat has undertaken some developmental activities in the village. It has contributed significantly in constructing the building of primary and high schools. It has sunk public wells for potable water for the villagers. Another noteworthy achievement of the Panchayat is the construction of pucca streets. Now, about three-fourth of the streets are pucca and the remaining kucha streets are to be made pucca soon. This improvement has helped, to a great extent, to maintain hygenic conditions in the village. This has virtually eliminited the mid-street foul deposits and pools of stagnant water in the streets. The Panchayat has also provided the streets with electric lamp-posts at certain places although these remain mostly out of order. Another achievement of the village Panchayat is the construction of new building for the dispensary and veterinary hospital in 1967 and 1983 respectively. Besides, the Gram Panchayat was instrumental in the construction of small bridges over rivulets and repair of the chaupals. However, the Gram Panchayat was a complete failure and has done nothing to propagate the various government plans relating to the development of agriculture and other allied activities in the village.

Cooperative Society : The village once was covered by a cooperative credit society. But the society which now stands defunct was liquidated for want of interest of its members and also the fraudulent and corrupt practices of the officials particularly the secretary. No subsequent attempt was made to revive the society at any time.

Ayurvedic Dispensary and Veterinary Hospital : The village has a Ayurvedic dispensary which was started in 1967 and is situated on one edge of the village. However, it is under the care of one B.M.S. doctor, a compounder/despenser and trained midwife. The dispensary attends all sorts of cases but it has no bed for indoor patients. The equipment and medicine in the dispensary are also limited and serious and complicated cases cannot be treated here. Therefore, the villagers have to go to Medical College and Hospital, Rohtak, for the treatment of such cases. It is another matter that it is not very inconvenient for the villagers to get the medical treatment at Rohtak. The Block Medical Officer is required to visit the dispensary frequently but comes only infrequently. There are also private medical practitioners who visit the village for their practice. There is a G.M.S. vaid who comes regularly to the village for the purpose. Besides, there are two untrained midwives belonging to Balmiki caste who are invariably called to handle delivery cases in the village. Despite the facilities available, some people in the village have also faith in *ojhas* for the cure for ailment and diseases. There are three such *ojhas* each one from Balmiki, Kumhar and Nai castes who are in some demand for the treatment of patients. However, there is no denying the fact that medical care over the years in the village has gradually gained in importance. Now, there is a large number of families that can afford to make use of town medical services. They are familiar with the Government hospital and with several private physicians in Rohtak city. It is to be admitted that public awareness regarding health in the village is not sound. There seems to be little information in the village regarding the prevention of disease and no noticeable attempt at prevention is made excepting the spraying of D.D.T. once in a while. There are huge open piles of cow-dung which can be seen all around the village. These are breeding centers for mosquitoes, flies and other harmful insects. However, malaria which was once accepted as inevitable and no one thought to get rid the village of it, is largely under control. Some other dreaded diseases like plague and small-pox which took endemic shape 40 years ago are completely eradicated from the face of the village.

The veterinary dispensary is also located in the same building which houses the Ayurvedic dispensary. This was started in the year 1983 in two rooms. It is manned by one stock-assistant and one helper. It was reported that there is more or less regular inoculation of animals in the village. But again for serious cases animals are brought to Rohtak for the right kind of treatment.

Post Office : Postal facilities are available in the village. The small post-office in the village was set up in 1965. It is housed in one room owned by a villager who is an ex-serviceman. The letters meant for villagers are distributed by the postman daily. On an average 30-40 letters per day are received in the village. This amply speaks of the rich contacts of the villagers with the world outside. Among other things, this also means that those who have migrated to other places maintain regular contacts with their family members behind. The post office has improved communication in the village and has made a great difference in the life of the villagers. Undoubtedly, the post office has played its part in the development of communication in the village. There is however no telephonic facility in the village.

Police Station : There is neither a police station nor a police outpost in the village. This is indicative of the fact that there is not much crime or disturbances in the village. The village falls under the jurisdiction of Rohtak city police station which is about 10 kilometers away. The village headman or the aggrieved party reports the matter to the station officer about any theft, crime, mishappening and other untoward occurrences that disturb peace in the village. During the year 1985-86, about 10 police cases were registered from this village.

Chaupals : The village Chaupal serves as the lodging place for marriage parties and also as a venue for meetings. There are three chaupals in the village. The Jat Chaupal is quite an old structure. It is a two storeyed building that can accommodate about 150 persons. The Saini Chaupal has a single storey with capacity for 100 persons. This was built about a decade ago. Another third Chaupal that of Harijans was constructed about 25 years back. It is small in size and not more than 50 persons can be accommodated. Significantly, all Chaupals were constructed with the financial contribution made by villagers themselves and without government help. Even in the case of Harijans' Chaupal government help remained nil.

Temples : The village has one Shivalya which is quite old. Recently, there came up another place of worship known as Baba Ka Dera. But only few persons pay their obeisance to these places. The Shivalya stands in the village on the northern side within the village boundary. The temple was constructed by the villagers' through donation about 100 years back. But now there seems to be no special arrangement made by the villagers for the care, maintenance and upkeep of the temple. It does not necessarily mean that people have lost faith in the deity. The villagers visit and throng the temple at Kiloi village, about two and a half kilometres away, to worship the deity Shivji. Fairs are held at Kiloi every year in the months of Sawan and Falgun to celebrate the occasion. The fairs connected with Shivji are organised with all pomp and show in the honour of the deity Shivji, and a large number of persons from the neighbouring villages including Ladhot participate in these.

Wells : Well plays a significant role in village life. Although water-supply scheme was introduced in the village in 1985 but wells continue to be the main source of water for the villagers for both drinking and washing purposes. Water supply to the village is made from the mainwater tank constructed at Makroli Kalan which is about two kilometres away. Water from the tank at Makroli Kalan is carried to Ladhot through steel pipes. But the water supply scheme is not working well. The villagers, in fact are also not in favour of the scheme as they are not in dire need of this. They are of the opinion that it is purely a wastage of money as the potable water is easily and sufficiently available from the village wells. Moreover, the sharing of water from the taps often resulted in disputes among the village women folk. As the scheme is unwanted, it is not well cared for and at places the taps are broken and missing. The villagers argue that the water supply scheme should be launched only in those problem villages where underground water is brackish and not fit for drinking.

There are seven wells in all which cater to the needs of different castes in the village. All these wells are located around the village within a radius of 250 metres. All the wells were built by the villagers themselves without government aid. There are four wells which are shared by all non-Scheduled Castes ; Scheduled Castes are not allowed to use these wells. However, there is no discrimination in the use of these wells as far as all non-Scheduled Castes like Jats, Brahmins, Sainis and other Backward Castes are concerned. It is obvious, therefore, that there is relaxation of caste rules and people are not rigid in matters of share of the wells. Scheduled Caste, Chamar and Balmiki have their separate exclusive wells. Surprisingly enough, these two castes do not share each other's well. Mostly the wells are on the edge of the village and near the habitat. The water capacity in these wells is adequate but during the hot summer season water level goes down and sometimes water gets scanty. The canal water, whenever convenient and necessary, is also used for other domestic purposes. There are also some old abandoned wells in the village which were dug long ago and now are out of use. The wells in the village provide an opportunity to the women-folk for assembling, gossiping, exchange of views and sharing each other experiences.

Ponds and Fields : The village has four ponds and all these are situated in the vicinity of the village. These ponds are identified by their names as Sunera, Bheri, Dharmshi and Sabiri. The main source of water to these ponds is the rain water. These ponds serve the village animals with drinking water all the year round. Sometimes, when rains are inadequate, then the water to these ponds is supplied and augmented with canal water. During the dry season the water becomes quite stinking and low which causes varied types of diseases to the animals.

The agricultural fields in the village are also identified with names and assume titles such as Pandu-wala, Bani, Sleta, Patain, Nala, Neem-Dhoba, Jungle, Dhanewala and Jhadfa. These stretches of land are located at a distance from the village within the radius of one and half kilometres.

Other Government Departments : Government has launched several rural programmes for the upliftment of rural population particularly the poor. In order to implement these programmes, certain government officials are directly associated with the village. Such important functionaries are : village revenue officer (Patwari), village level worker (Gram-sewak) and agriculture inspector.

There are two Patwaris in the village—one who deals with all matters relating to land and the other who collects irrigation charges from the cultivators. They are whole time officials of the government in the village. The main function of the village *Patwari* (village Revenue official) is to maintain accounts and record of every plot of land within the revenue area of the village. He enters in his documents any change in land ownership caused due to death and other reasons with a statement of the rights of each heir of land. He notes transfers and alterations in legal rights of land.

There is also one village level worker (Gram-Sewak), who is at the base of the bureaucratic hierarchy and on whom the success of the Community Development Programme largely depends. But his contribution in the village was hardly visible. Many people in the village even do not know, much less recognise their Gram-Sewak. However, people are aware of their block and in fact the word block is a part of the village vocabulary. It is the service arm of the government and is to render to the villagers whatever advice or help is needed by them. But the benefits expected to accrue from block activities are availed of mostly by the rich and few privileged households of the village. The purpose of the block is to provide every village with an opportunity to produce more, to earn more, to consume more, and—as a result—to enjoy better living. But all this can be achieved only if the village level workers deputed to help the villagers feel concerned and interested.

The institution of *Lambardar*, beyond any doubt, is very important. There are two Lambardars namely Dalip and Ram Dass in the village. Their main duty is to collect land revenue and *chullah* tax from the villagers. Lambardars are paid out of the land revenue thus collected. They also serve as attestation authorities in verifying the antecedents of the villagers.

Chowkidar is at the lowest rung of the hierarchy. There are two chowkidars in the village. Both belong to Balmiki caste. They are paid at the rate of Rs. 150 per month. Village Lambardars make arrangement for their payment. But for the last four years, it has been alleged, that these chowkidars have not been paid even this pittance. They have represented their cases to different quarters but to no avail. Chowkidar performs the duties of watchman at night and also serves as an attendent to the government officials who are permanently employed in the village or who occasionally visit the village.

Caste Structure

Like most Indian villages, caste is the central factor in the life of Ladhot. For this very reason, we have carried out our analysis of the village in terms of caste. Caste is a significant unit of social structure and performs many important functions in the organization of the village. The customs followed by some castes are generally different in some respects from those of the other castes.

A caste is a collection of families bearing the same name, generally associated with a specific occupation and claiming common descent from a mythological ancestor. Each one is born in a particular caste and he cannot get out of it. Each caste has its particular occupation and its own customs which often determine even the minutest details of daily life. Inter-caste marriages are strictly restricted within their own parent castes. No doubt, the caste system based on religious beliefs and sanction is slowly breaking. Many factors have been responsible for this gradual change and decaying influence of the caste system which we will examine in detail in Chapter 4.

The village Ladhot represents 15 castes each having a distinct character. The Jat, Saini, Brahman, Chamar and Balmiki in that order are numerically five important castes in the village. The other castes in the village are Ahir, Punjabi, Baniya, Lohar, Sunar, Khati, Nai, Kumhar, Doom and Bairagi. All these castes, excepting Doom, belong to Hindu religion. The religion followed by Doom families is Muslim. An important feature of life in the village is segergations of castes, by area of residence, in eating, and for the most part in social interactions. Now, we briefly describe the castes in this village.

Ahir : There are only two households belonging to this caste. Ahirs also called Yadavs, are said to be the descendants of Lord Krishna. Ahir, which is an important caste, found in southern part of Haryana, makes a very good farmer and a soldier.

Brahmin : Brahman is an upper caste. This caste has 31 households with a population of 8.5 per cent of the entire village. It is a caste which is still considered socially superior though much of the aura attached with it has decayed over the passage of time. The caste which was considered exclusively a priestly class is now engaged in agriculture and other occupations. Brahmins in Ladhot own lands and are mostly the peasants.

Jats : Jat in the village is numerically a dominant caste with 153 families and make 46.6 per cent of the total population. Jats, who are settled mostly in Haryana, Punjab, Uttar Pradesh and Rajasthan, also fall in the upper stratum of Hindu society. These are stated to be the original settlers of the village. They are traditionally agriculturists and warriors. They make a good farmer and their agriculture practices are good within the means at their disposal.

Saini : Sainis traditionally are vegetable growers. However, in Ladhot, the Sainis are farmers and no more given to growing vegetables than other farmers. The Saini caste is the third largest group with 33 families and nearly 10 per cent of the population. They are a land-owning caste.

Baniya : Baniyas belong to the money-lending class. There is only one family of Baniya in the village. This family has no land and is engaged in shop-keeping.

Punjabi : Punjabi, in fact, is not a caste but it is a term coined at the time of partition of the country in 1947 and continued to remain in usage. All those families who migrated from Pakistan during that upheaval are called Punjabis. There is only one such family settled in the village and engaged in shop-keeping. There are also three other shops of Punjabis but their families do not stay in the village. They come to the village daily from Rohtak city to run their business only.

Khati (*Carpenter*) : The number of Khati families in the village is eight. This is a service caste which constructs houses, wooden tools and implements for other castes. The Khati caste presents the picture of declining business due to the increased outside contacts of the villagers. Previously, their workshop used to be full of activities and had sufficient amount of work to go about. But now they have taken to different work in and outside the village. They do not own land barring one family whose piece of land hardly measures one-fourth hectare.

Kumhars (Potter) : There are seven families of this caste in this village. Kumhar is a Jajmani caste and traditional occupation of its members is to supply earthen pots of their patrons on ceremonial occasions.

Lohar (Blacksmith) : Lohars are craftsmen serving mainly the farmers. There are 13 families of Lohar in the village. The families are serviceable to the agriculturists and prepare simple agriculture implements which include Dranti, Khurpa and Plough Blades. Some Lohar families have migrated to other places and have also taken to agriculture. They have suffered due to the increased city contacts of the farmers who prefer and acquire agricultural implements mostly from the city. The Lohar families, left in the village, are struggling hard for their livelihood and are always prepared to accept whatever job or work they lay their hands upon.

Nai (Barber) : There are three families of Nai caste. A Nai family serves on the occasions of birth, marriage, death and other religious and ritual occasions. A male member of the caste shaves the beard and gets the hair cut of male members of his jajman family. A female member of the caste washes the heads of women-folk. Both male and female Nai render essential services at the time of marriage, birth of a child and other occasions mentioned above. A Nai has to give invitation on behalf of the host to the villagers and call them when preparations for the ceremony get ready.

Sunar (Goldsmith) : There are three families of the goldsmith in the village. These three families of goldsmith earn their livelihood by preparing and selling ornaments to the villagers.

Bairagi : The number of households of Bairagi in the village is seven. They are not endowed with land but are engaged in the cultivation of land which they arrange on lease. They are also engaged as agricultural labour in the village and factory workers in the city to earn their livings.

Doom : There are 13 families of this caste in the village. The Ladhot Dooms are Muslims. All these households are landless and earn their livelihood by working as agricultural workers and factory workers and by singing songs to the villagers for their entertainment. Dooms in the village appear to be separated from the majority of their fellow villagers by a barrier of religion as well as of caste. They are all settled in cluster on the eastern edge of the village. Dooms in the village have now adopted many customs and rites of the Hindus and participate in common village activities. The peculiar thing about Dooms is that these families in the village are accorded a position higher than Scheduled Castes. They may sit and share on the same cot with other superior castes but Scheduled Castes dare not to do so.

Scheduled Castes : There are two Scheduled Castes viz. Chamar and Balmiki in the village. These castes have been given the status of Scheduled Castes in our Constitution. The groups mentioned in the Constitution of India as meriting particular favour in view of their social and economic oppressed position. They are the outcastes of traditional Indian society. They are also known as Harijan(s), a denomination by Mahatma Gandhi, meaning 'the people of God'. The British had earlier coined the term 'untouchables' to describe the same group. They are service castes The number of households of these two castes in the village runs to 95 and they occupy quite a significant place in the village life.

Chamars are leather workers and some of them still follow their traditional occupation. Others have turned into agriculture labour in the village as they do not own land. They also find a good deal of outside employment due to the reservation policy of government. Significantly, Chamars are economically better off than the Balmikis. This clearly proves that compared with the Balmikis, Chamars have taken more advantage of the concession and reservasions provided by the government. Currently, the well off Chamars do not want their castemen to do such menial jobs for others as are demeaning in nature.

Balmiki is the caste despised the most. Even among the Scheduled Castes, this caste gets the lowest ranking. The local nomenclature of this caste varies from place to place such as Balmiki, Chura and Bhangi. Balmikis, like several other castes in the village, do not own any land. They are supposed to perform varied types of odd jobs which no one else in the village does. They are at once the agricultural workers and scavengers of the village. They raise poultry and tame swines to supplement their income.They dispose of the dead animals of the village only for their skin, and perform some other similar jobs. Their women-folk, besides acting as scavengers, also act as untrained midwives for the family where a child is born. The despised position of this caste sill persists.

CHAPTER 3

VILLAGE ECONOMY

Before attempting to design any developmental programme and strategy for the village it is necessary to understand the nature and type of the village economy. This chapter, therefore, deals with some important economic characteristics of this village. Importantly, the economic life in the village revolves round agriculture and thus development of agriculture is sine-qua-non for the growth of the village economy. This chapter is divided in three sections. Section one deals with village population and its various characteristics. Section two describes the village land, agriculture and their other related aspects. Section three provides, inter-alia, important economic aspects of the village economy such as ownership of assest, occupational pattern, unemployment, savings and debt problems.

I

Households and Population

Some information in respect of population of the village has already been provided in the preceding chapter. It is intended in this section to furnish detailed information on this aspect. The castes of Ladhot along with the number of households and population are set out in Table 3.1.

It is evident, from Table 3.1 that the village is multi-caste having as many as 15 castes. The caste composition in the village is quite heterogeneous. Jats having 153 households and 1091 individuals is numerically the dominant caste. In terms of percentages Jats occupy a little more than 41 per cent of the total households and share 46 per cent of the total population. The next largest group is that of Scheduled Castes comprising Chamars and Balmikis. Scheduled Castes alone own 25.6 per cent of the households and form 22.6 per cent of the population in the village. The Scheduled Castes are subservient to the other castes in the sense that they supply labour and perform all odd jobs mosty to other castes. The Saini caste is the third largest group sharing 8.9 per cent of the households and nearly 10 per cent of the population. Brahmin is the close fourth with 31 households and having 8.4 per cent of the total village population. The remaining 10 other castes share among themselves merely 13 per cent of the village population. Clearly, the position of these 10 castes in respect of number is not significant in the village ; it being quite negligible in case of Ahir, Baniya, Punjabi, Sonar and Nai where the number of households in any single caste does not exceed three.

Population by Sex and Age

It can be observed from Table 3.2 that there is variation in six ratio. There is an excess of male over the female population. The sex-wise composition of the village population reveals that for every 100 males, there are 77 females. Interestingly enough, female population outnumber males in almost all the castes. The difference between the number of males and females is unlikely to have occurred by chance. There are a number of conceivable reasons for this situation. One important reason for the male population having a numerical edge over females can be explained in terms of high infant mortality rate among the latter due to insufficient attention and care given to girls after birth. Besides, social and economic factors still continue to work against female.

TABLE 3.1

Distribution of Households Population Castewise

Caste	Number of Households	Percentage to Total Households	Population in Number	Percentage to Total Population
Ahir	3	0.8	14	0.6
Brahmin	31	8.4	199	8.4
Jat	153	41.3	1091	46.0
Saini	33	8.9	230	9.7
Baniya	1	0.2	6	0.3
Punjabi	1	0.2	4	0.2
Khati	8	2.2	47	2.0
Kumhar	7	1.9	35	1.5
Lohar	13	3.5	57	2.4
Nai	3	0.8	21	0.8
Sonar	3	0.8	21	0.8
Bairagi	7	1.9	33	1.4
Doom	13	3.5	78	3.3
Chamar	45	12,1	246	10.4
Balmiki	50	13.5	290	12.2
Total	371	100.0	2372	100.0

Note : The ranking of castes that has been used is purely alphabetical in their own group and not a guide to status of the various castes in the village. However, on the basis of socio-economic conditions and the status provided by the government, the castes may be classified into three categories viz., upper castes, backward classes and scheduled castes. Ahir, Brahmin, Jat, Saini, Baniya, Punjabi, Sonar belong to the upper castes. Khati, Kumhar, Lohar, Nai, Bairagi and Doom are termed backward castes. Scheduled castes include Chamar and Balmiki in the village.

Another important characteristic of population is the distribution of population between adult and minor. The figures in the same table indicate that the proportion of minor population (below 15 years) is nearly 45 per cent. This high proportion of children only reflects a large number of unproductive consumers. The principal reason for a higher child-population in the village obviously lies in the high birth rate. It is essential, therefore, to bring down further the birth rate in order to reduce the non-productive consumers in the village. The rising population, undoubtedly, is a drag on scarce economic resources available to the villagers. Its negative impact is felt in a variety of ways. A high and expanding population of children increases the burden of the care of the young through nutrition, medical care, public health, education and housing.

Family Size

It hardly needs emphasis that family is the basic unit of organization in the village life. It is evident from Table 3.3 that the average family size for the entire village works out to be 6.4 persons. As among the various castes, however, the size deviated substantially from this average. Jat and Saini, the two major castes, report larger family size than this average. Understandably, the main reason for this lies in the fact that these castes live as joint families more in number as compared to other castes. Joint family is explained as one where members of the lineage live together with the females and children and share in common the hearth, wealth and shelter. It consists of the elders, husband-wife, their married sons, unmarried children, and their married son's children. Though the joint family is the characteristic feature of our tradition in the village Ladhot, the system is sadly on the way out. Joint family system is disintegrating fast giving way to the nuclear type of families which usually comprises husband-wife and unmarried children. We observed that joint families are mostly prevalent among the land owning castes like Jats and Sainis. It appears that joint family is a characteristic of landed community and is a product of an agrarian economy. Land keeps the family structurally united. The farming family lives together in the interest of the landed property and to keep it intact and safe. Among the non-farming castes particularly the Scheduled

TABLE 3.2

Distribution of Population by Sex and Age

Caste	Sex		Age		Total
	Males	Females	Adult	Minor	
Ahir	9	5	7	7	14
Brahmin	105	94	124	75	199
Jat	622	469	631	460	1091
Saini	132	98	133	97	230
Baniya	3	3	2	4	6
Punjabi	3	1	2	2	4
Khati	30	17	22	25	47
Kumhar	17	18	14	21	35
Lohar	33	24	27	30	57
Nai	11	10	8	13	21
Sonar	12	9	13	8	21
Bairagi	18	15	22	11	33
Doom	41	37	47	31	78
Chamar	137	109	132	114	246
Balmiki	162	128	129	161	290
Total	1335	1037	1313	1059	2372
Percentage	56.3	43.7	55.4	44.6	100.00

TABLE 3.3

Family Size

Caste	Average Number of Persons per Family
Ahir	4.7
Brahmin	6.4
Jat	7.1
Saini	7.0
Baniya	6.0
Punjabi	4.0
Khati	5.9
Kumhar	5.0
Lohar	4.4
Nai	7.0
Sonar	7.0
Bairagi	4.7
Doom	6.0
Chamar	5.5
Balmiki	5.8
Average	6.4

Castes, nuclear families are mostly prevalent. Thus, it can safely be concluded that predominance of joint families in case of land owning households is the result of compelling circumstances and there is nothing voluntary about it.

II

This section deals with village land and other related issues. The most important factor which influences village economy is the agricultural land, its ownership pattern and mode of use. A fair knowledge of these is vital for understanding the various facets, problems and prospects of village life. Hence, the study that follows dilates upon land, its ownership, and use in terms of crops and their allocation patterns. The starting point in the whole discussions obviously would be to present a picture of the dimensions of land in terms of what the villagers have and can possibly have. This is to be examined both in terms of its existing availability and use, as also the possibilities of augmenting this scarce resource through land management measures.

Land Area and Uses

Of the total 671 hectares geographical area of the village the land under cultivation is 590 hectares which forms 87.9 per cent of the total area. Evidently there is very little scope for the extension of area under cultivation. However, efforts can still be made to bring some extra land under plough. Such efforts, no doubt, would require costly investment as these lands have remained barren (*banjar*) for the last many years. Also due to the increasing demand of land for non-agricultural uses, the prospects on extensive margin appear to be quite dim. More and more land currently under cultivation may get used up for constructing houses and other purposes. It is also feared that more and more land may turn unfit for cultivations because of the adverse effect of the alkaline and saline contents in the soil and water-logging in some fields in

TABLE 3.4

Land Area and Uses-1981

	Land Uses	Area (in Hectares)	Percentage
(A)	Land available for cultivation	590	87.9
(B)	Non-Cultivated Land	81	12.1
(i)	Land not cultivated for 20 yrs. (Banjar Kadimi)	21	3.1
(ii)	Non-cultivated for more than three years	4	0.6
(iii)	Non-cultivable due to flood water logging and salinity (Thur)	3	0.4
(iv)	Common (Samlati) land including habitat	53	7.9
	Total area of the village (A+B)	671	100.00

Source : Village Land Records.

the village. The land reported unfit for cultivation by the cultivators as revealed during the course of Survey, works out 213 hectares which far exceeds the area shown in the Patwari's records. This gives a very dismal picture of land quality in the village which warrants immediate attention for its reclamation and improvement. It is more or less clear that there exists no scope for the additional land which can be brought under cultivation in the village. In view of this tight situation, it is urgently needed to add to the land resource on its intensive margin, i.e., by increasing the intensity of cultivation and making improvement on the existing cultivated land. The priority should, therefore, be accorded to accelerate the intensity of crops which has not yet reached to its limit in the village. Another line of action to augment the land resource is to make the best use of existing available land and manage it judiciously and carefully. Such steps would both prevent the exhaustion of its capabilities and add to its productive capacity. This, we all know, would require money and other concerted measures such as soil testing, proper ploughing and seeding, replacement of the used-up ingredients of the soil, adequate fertilization through both organic and inorganic manures etc. An optimum use of land through proper cropping schedule and pattern needs to be evolved. The use of the high yielding varieties of seeds, combined with adequate dosage of complementary inputs is equally necessary if efforts at improving soils are to make any dent.

Irrigation

Irrigation facilities appear to be adequate on many farms in terms of Command area. But in actual fact it is not so. Table 3.5 gives the irrigation position source-wise :

TABLE 3.5
Area Under Irrigation

Source of Irrigation	Hectares	Percentage
Government Canal	503	85.3
Tubewells	3	0.5
Wells and Tubewells	9	1.5
Total area under Irrigation	515	87.3
Non-irrigated area (Barani)	75	12.7

Table 3.5 depicts that the Command area under irrigation is 87.3 per cent of the total cultivated area and the area non-irrigated is only 12.7 per cent. Of the area irrigated, canal accounts for a major share and the insignificant residual is being shared by wells and tubewells. Evidently, canal emerges as the principal source of water supply in the village. But it is to be noted very carefully that the irrigated area shown is not the area irrigated effectively but only the Command area which makes all the difference. It does not reveal watering frequency according to the requirement of crops. This tends to lead to erroneous impression regarding the irrigation facilities in the village. Effective irrigation facilities as reported by the farmers are not sufficient as are made out to be in the record. Moreover, during the course of enquiry, the total land under irrigation as reported by the cultivators worked out only 435 hectares which is much less than shown in village records.

Landless and Land-Owning Households

Mention has already been made regarding the total land availability in the village. Land is the major means of production in the village where the overwhelming majority of households depend for their living. The picture relating to the landless and land owning households in the village is presented through Table 3.6.

It is evident from Table 3.6 that 158 households in the village (42.6 per cent) do not own any land. They have to depend largely on wage work. Out of 15 castes in the village, only 6 castes own land. It is also noticed that two castes, namely Brahmin and Jat between them command 92.2 per cent of the total village agricultural land. After Brahmin and Jat, Saini caste which constitutes 13.7 per cent of the land owning households account for 7.4 per cent of the total land. The other three landowning castes namely Ahir, Lohar and Khati put together share only 0.4 per cent of the entire land.

Size of Holding and Fragmentation

In order to carry out our analysis further and to complete the land picture, we turn our attention to the question of size of land holding and the problem of fragmentation.

TABLE 3.6

Number of Landless and Land Owning Households

Caste	Landless	Land Owning	Percentage of Households Owning Land	Land Owned (in Hectares)	Percentage of Village Land
Ahir	2	1	0.4	1.0	0.17
Brahmin	2	29	13.7	63.9	10.80
Jat	1	152	71.4	480.1	81.40
Saini	4	29	13.7	43.6	7.40
Baniya	1	—	—	—	—
Punjabi	1	—	—	—	—
Khati	7	1	0.4	0.2	0.03
Kumhar	7	—	—	—	—
Lohar	12	1	0.4	1.2	0.20
Nai	3	—	—	—	—
Sonar	3	—	—	—	—
Bairagi	7	—	—	—	—
Doom	13	—	—	—	—
Chamar	45	—	—	—	—
Balmiki	50	—	—	—	—
Total percentage	158	213	100.0	590.0	100.00

TABLE 3.7

Differential Land Holdings

(Number of Households Owning Land)

Caste	Land per Cultivating Household (in Hectares)	Less than 1.0 Hectares	Between 2-5 Hectares	Above 5 Hectares
Ahir	1.0	1	—	—
Brahmin	2.2	23	5	1
Jat	3.2	90	42	20
Saini	1.5	24	4	1
Baniya	—	—	—	—
Punjabi	—	—	—	—
Khati	0.2	1	—	—
Kumhar	—	—	—	—
Lohar	1.2	1	—	—
Nai	—	—	—	—
Sonar	—	—	—	—
Bairagi	—	—	—	—
Doom	—	—	—	—
Chamar	—	—	—	—
Balmiki	—	—	—	—
Weighted Average/ Total	2.8	140	51	22

Table 3.7 gives brief but a vivid account of the size of holdings in the village. The average size of holding for the village, as a whole, works out to be 2.8 hectares. The average size of 3.2 hectares is the highest in case of Jat and the lowest 0.2 hectares for Khati. The distribution of land in terms of size is highly uneven and skewed. There is preponderance of small holdings measuring below 2 hectares in size. The small sized holding numbering 140 constitute more than three-fifths of the holdings but possess hardly one-third of the agricultural land. On the other end, there are only 22 big land owning households accounting for more than 41 per cent of the total agricultural land in the village. Thus, there is obviously a small minority of the peasantry whose size of holdings exceeds 5 hectares. Remaining households who occupy positions between these two categories of households may be termed as medium sized cultivators. It should be emphasised here that the distribution of land within each caste is extremely uneven and the membership of a caste well-endowed with land, such as the Jats is no guarantee that an individual household of that caste will also be well endowed. There are 90 Jat families i.e. 58.8 per cent of the total households whose size of holding is below the village average holding. Although many Jats do not have economic and Viable holdings yet by virtue of their number they enjoy dominance of the ownership of land in the village.

It is discovered further that not only the size of holdings in the village is small but these are also fragmented. Although, after the consolidation of holdings, (a measure of land reforms) the number of land fragments for the entire village has been reduced from 743 to 545 but still the number is far from the desired level. Number of fragments per average holding in terms of three sized groups are 2.3, 3.1 and 3.3 respectively. It is observed that the number of fragments increases with an increase in the size of holding showing a direct movement between the two. These small parcels of one's holding can be seen in the form of tiny plots scattered all around the village in different directions. Fragmentation is a continuing process in Indian agriculture which takes place largely due to the subdivision of landed property among joint owners, each of whom wants a share in each quality of the ancestral land. As a consequence, in this process, the unit of cultivation in many cases gets reduced to such a tiny size that cultivation is rendered uneconomic and sometimes impossible. The smallness of the holding size is an hindrance in the use of improved agricultural practices such as better seeds, use of superior agricultural machinery, construction of wells and tubewells, fencing of land and other improvements on the land. Excessive fragmentation has also resulted in the wastage of land in boundaries and fencing. Sometimes quarrels over boundaries of small plots lead to litigation. In view of the difficult problem, it may aptly be surmised that if agriculture is to survive then the mounting problems of sub-division and fragmentation, caused by the rapid increase in rural population and breaking up of the joint family system, must be overcome squarely.

Tenancy

Tenancy is a legacy in village agriculture which requires a closer analysis. Tenancy implies the system of leasing of land which reflects the normative demand side of the land in the village. Table3.8 enables us to analyse the tenancy dynamics of different categories of farmers.

A very startling picture of land tenancy is revealed in the village. The extent of tenancy is quite wide despite the land reform measures which are aimed at to discourage it. More than one-half (51%) of the total agricultural land of Ladhot is put under tenancy which is not shown in the record. It may, however, be noted that tenancy in Ladhot is not confined to the same caste both for land owners and tenants. An attempt to examine the extent of tenancy to identify the size classes of net leasers-out and leasers-in would yield interesting results. The net area leased by the small farmers was more than one-half of the land owned by them. The position of medium farmers was more or less akin to that of small farmers and the land leased-in by them equalled nearly one-half the size of their own land. Large sized cultivators also, contrary to the belief held, lease in land quite substantially. Of the total 300.4 hectares of land leased in by all categories of farmers in the village, 122.8 hectares (40.9 per cent) was leased-in by the large farmers alone. Of the total land leased out

TABLE 3.8

Extent of Tenancy in 1985

(in hectares)

Size of Holding	Cultivating Households (Number)	Land Owned	Land Leased In	Land Leased Out
Small	140	193.0	107.3	161.1
	(65.7)	(32.7)	(35.7)	(53..5)
Medium	51	154.6	70.3	96.8
	(23.9)	(26.2)	(23.4)	(32.2)
Large	22	242.1	122.8	42.9
	(10.4)	(41.1)	(40.9)	(14.3)
Total	213	589.7	300.4	300.8

Note : The figures in parentheses denote percentages.

in the village, the share of each category of farmers in that order works out 53.5, 32.6 and 14.3 per cent, respectively. If we collate these two aspects of tenancy viz., leased-in and leased-out, then some interesting results would emerge. Small farmes turn out to be the net lessors-out in terms of land area. More or less the same position is noticeable in respect of medium-sized holdings. But in case of large holdings, the situation gets reversed where the area leased-in is almost three times the area leased-out by them. Therefore, on the whole, there occurred a net transfer of land from the small and medium farmers to the large ones. The reasons for such a situation are not difficult to explain.

The major reason has been that the big farmers resume self-culivation due to profitability as also for fear of tenancy laws. There is widespread fear among the big farmers that the leasing out of land will put their ownership title at risk. The temptation to resume land for self-cultivation has also become intense in the wake of technological breakthrough in agriculture. On the other hand, the small farmers, who are in services and other professions at far away places, do not cultivate land themselves. Because of the very smallness of the size of their holdings, and the circumstances detailed above, they are compelled to abandon cultivation. And the alternative left for them is either to sell the land or to lease it out. Selling of land is the last resort in the village as farmers cling to mother earth emotionally. Consequently, all such land is put under tenancy. The small farmers, who stay at village for lack of outside job avenues become land hungry and try to acquire more land to eke-out their living and also to make better use of their abundant fixed farm resources like family and bullock labour.

As regards the problem of tenancy in the village, it is necessary to elaborate further the mode of payment by the tenant. Tenancy in Ladhot takes two forms, namely, share cropping (*Batai*) and fixed annual rent (*Bhada*). In case of the first, the gross produce and its by-product is divided equally between the landowner and the tenant. The landowner would also share some expenses incurred by the tenant for raising the crop. According to the later arrangement, some monetary rent is fixed which is paid by the tenant in one or two instalments during the year. The prevalent rent in the village depends on the quality and location of land. This ranges between Rs. 1500 to 3500 per hectare per annum.

It needs to be highlighted that the leasing contracts are often under hand, always in oral form with terms and conditions that suited land owners. This practice is possible because of the monopolistic situation in land market where the seekers of land have no alternative avenues of income or employment. And, therefore, any attempt to make the tenant owner of the land or the slogan 'Land to the tiller' is thwarted. There had been not even a single case in Ladhot where a tenant became the owner of the land. Besides, tenants do not try to become owner of the land knowing-fully that they cannot easily establish their claims to the ownership of such land. If an attempt of this kind is made by any tenant then he will surely never get the land on lease again in the whole village. It was also revealed that leases are of short duration (generally for one year) mostly on oral contracts as already indicated. Under the situation, the tenant can neither claim the ownership of land nor can he disclose the fact of the lease to government due to the fear that he may not get land on lease in future. And the result has been that illegal tenancy goes on unchecked in the village with mutual consent of the land owners and the tenants.

Distribution of Land

In more recent years, the question of re-distribution of agricultural land has assumed significance. We now summarize the major distributive aspects of the agricultural land in the village through Table 3.8. The table reveals that land distribution is far from equal. Land is greatly concentrated in a handful of cultivating households. On the one end, the large farmers having holdings measuring 5 hectares or more, constitute 10 per cent of the peasantry but command more than 40 per cent of the village agricultural land. On the other end, the small farmers owning holdings upto 2 hectares constitute nearly 66 per cent of the cultivators but possess even less than 33 per cent of the total land. In between these two are the medium sized farmers who constitute about 24 perc ent of the households accounting for 26 per cent of the owned area. The inequality in distribution of land is also illustrated with the help of Lorenz curve shom below in Fig. 1. The illustration, no doubt, would have been much fruitful had the past data also been made available for the purpose of making comparison between two or more periods. But the required information could not be secured. It is clear that the line of actual distribution is away from the line of equal distribution implying, that there is inequal distribution of land in the village. The greater is the distance between the curve and line of equal distribution the greater will be the dispersion and so the greater inequality in land distribution.

It may be emphasised that the ceiling law (Ceiling of Land Holding Act, 1957) to mop up the surplus land has had on effect on land distribution in the village. There is not even a single family from the village whose land was lost due to ceiling. It also means that there was no surplus land in the village

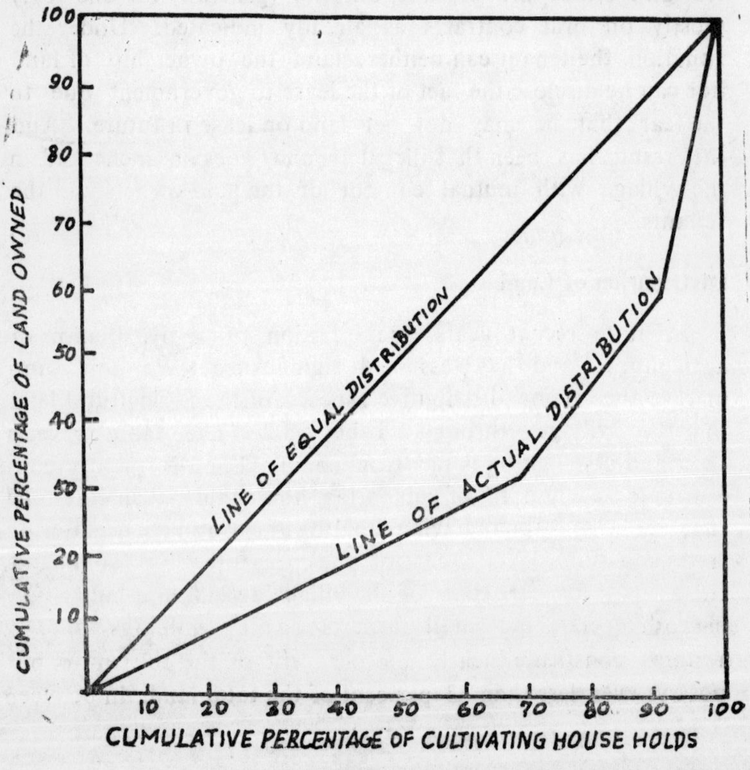

which could be distributed among the landless or small farmers. There is, however, no denying the fact that a more equitable distribution of land is desirable in view of the scarcity of this material resource. It, however, goes without saying that it should not be done indiscriminately. The doubts raised about the wisdom of breaking up large holding (not so large now) on economic grounds are valid. Application of modern machines and inputs are only possible on economically viable farms. Alternatively stated, the new agricultural technologies are heavily biased in favour of large holdings. The breaking up of the holdings any further would result not only in lowering of agricultural produce but also in dissipating the scarce agricultural resources. The landless and marginal farmers should be benefited by good wages and some other rural programmes and certainly not by giving them land or extra land. This seems to be the only rational strategy left with us now. Many studies conducted in several states have clearly established that beneficiaries of ceiling did not do well with the land given to them. This was partly on account of the lack of management and skill on their part and also to the failure of several agencies to assist these new cultivators with some preferential programmes.

Cropping Pattern

Cropping pattern means the allocation of total cropped area under different crops at a point of time. It has great significance in that it reveals the demand pattern of crops to which it responds. In any plan for cropping pattern or any change in the existing cropping pattern, it is essential that we acquire a knowledge of the existing situation, as also its history and the influences that shape it. This type of analysis is expected to reveal the possibilities of a desired change in cropping patterns as also the limits on them. We analyse below in somc details the important characteristics of the cropping pattern followed by cultivators in the village.

A close look at the Tables 3.9 (a), 3.9 (b) and 3.9 (c) brings out at once the important features of the cropping pattern. These are : two distinct agricultural seasons, distribution of crops between major and minor crops, diversified pattern, food

TABLE 3.9 (a)

Nature of Crop Pattern During Kharif Seasons

(in hectares)

Crops Kharif	1968	1973	1978	1983	1985
Rice	77 (11.2)	39 (4.7)	97 (11.0)	44 (4.7)	63 (9.7)
Jowar	63 (9.2)	113 (13.6)	119 (13.6)	184 (19.8)	53 (8.2)
Bajra	18 (2.6)	87 (10.6)	110 (12.5)	126 (13.6)	14 (2.2)
Sugarcane	73 (10.7)	84 (10.1)	80 (9.1)	82 (8.8)	44 (6.8)
Cotton	10 (1.5)	7 (0.8)	6 (0.7)	2 (0.2)	5 (0.8)
Jute	—	2 (0.2)	1 (0.1)	3 (0.3)	1 (0.2)
Gowar	5 (0.7)	16 (1.9)	16 (1.8)	12 (1.3)	4 (0.6)
Maize	1 (0.1)	1 (0.1)	—	—	—
Vegetable oil	—	—	—	1 (0.1)	—
Vegetables	—	—	—	—	—
Janter	4 (0.6)	—	—	11 (1.2)	2 (0.3)
Dal	—	—	—	11 (1.2)	—
Kharif Total	251 (36.6)	349 (42.0)	429 (48.8)	476 (51.2)	186 (28.8)

TABLE 3.9 (b)
Nature of Crop Pattern During Rabi Seasons

(in hectares)

Crops Rabi	1968		1973		1978		1983		1985	
Wheat	218	(81.7)	350	(42.1)	325	(36.9)	403	(43.7)	389	(60.3)
Barley	58	(8.5)	20	(2.4)	18	(2.0)	12	(1.3)	3	(0.5)
Gram	46	(6.7)	47	(5.7)	42	(4.8)	3	(0.3)	14	(2.2)
Wheat Gram	11	(1.6)	10	(1.2)	7	(0.8)	1	(0.1)	6	(1.0)
Sarson	2	(0.3)	7	(0.8)	6	(0.7)	5	(0.5)	17	(2.6)
Barseem	17	(2.5)	14	(1.7)	12	(1.4)	17	(1.8)	19	(2.9)
Methi+Gram	20	(2.9)	6	(0.7)	25	(2.8)	6	(0.6)	7	(1.1)
Barley	6	(0.9)	—		16	(1.8)	—		—	
Masoor	1	(0.1)	—		—		—		—	
Toria	—		—		—		—		—	
Wheat+Barley	.—		—		—		—		—	
Mator	56	(8.2)	28	(3.4)	—		—		—	
Vegetables	—		—		—		—		—	
Safeda	—		—		—		—		—	
Garden	—		—		—		4	(0.4)	4	(0.6)
Rabi Total	435	(63.4)	482	(58.0)	451	(51.2)	451	(48.7)	459	(71.2)
Grand Total area Kharif and Rabi	686		831		880		927		645	

TABLE 3.9 (c)

Major Features of Crop Pattern

(in hectares)

	1968	1973	1978	1983	1985
Food Crops	374 (54.5)	530 (63.8)	581 (66.0)	590 (63.6)	486 (75 3)
Non-Food Crops	199 (29.0)	152 (18.3)	111 (12.6)	118 (12.7)	76 (11.8)
Fodder	113 (16.5)	149 (17.9)	188 (21.5)	219 (23.7)	83 (12.9)
Intensity of Cropping	128	156	163	170	117
*High Yielding Varieties (HYV)	—	—	—	—	430 (92)
Crops Wasted	113 (16.5)	92 (11.1)	240 (27.3)	246 (26.5)	9 (1.4)

Note : Figures in parentheses in all the three tables 3.9 (a), 3.9 (b) and 3.9 (c) are percentages to total cropped area.

*High yielding varieties of wheat, rice and bajra.

crops versus non-food crops, intensity of cropping and high yielding crops and crops wasted. We proceed to discuss all these breifly in that order.

Crop Seasons: There are two agricultural seasons viz, Khar i and Rabi in the village. Kharif season starts usually in June or July and Rabi in October and November. The harvesting of Kharif crops takes place in September-October and Rabi crops in April and May. The preparation of fields for the subsequent season begins soon after the harvest. The farmers of Ladhot, like other farmers elsewhere in Haryana, wait for the onset of the monsoon rains for sowing their Kharff crops. Very often, because of poor summer rains, Kharif sowing gets late making it difficult to sow the second crop during Rabi. This, however, is not necessary to be so in case of those farmers who have adequate and assured irrigation facilities on their farms. The major Kharif crops of the village include rice, jowar, bajra and sugarcane.* The major Rabi crops are wheat, barley, gram, barseem and sarson. Regarding the allocation of cropped land according to seasons, Rabi season has an edge over the Kharif season in terms of the area sown. A time series analysis from 1968 to 1985 would show that the percentage of the total cropped area under Kharif has fluctuated between 28.8 per cent (1985), the lowest to 51.2 per cent the highest in 1983. And the area allotted to Rabi crops works at to be 48.7 per cent the lowest and 71.2 the highest in the corresponding periods. The land utilization and the wide fluctuations in case of Kharif crops are explained in terms of the monsoon rains which make a decisive influence in the matter of land use. If these rains are scanty or untimely then farmers would prefer to keep their land fallow and wait till the arrival of the Rabi season. In fact, the farmers give more preference to Rabi crops particularly to wheat and sarson which are relatively high valued crops.

Diversified Pattern : It is easily noticeable that the crop pattern in the village is not of monoculture or even of twin-culture type. It is, instead, quite diversified in that a wide variety of crops, which compete for space and other farm

*Sugarcane is a full year crop.

resources are grown. There are as many as 21 crops or crop mix which are raised during the cycle year. In terms of the percentage of total cultivated area under each crop, five overlapping categories of crops can be classified as the major crops, the minor crops, food crops, non-food crops and fodder crops. The major crops of the village are wheat, rice, jowar, bajra and sugarcane while other crops may be termed as minor crops. The four major crops of the village are cultivated nearly on 85 per cent of the total cropped area and thus are quite important. Wheat, a staple food crop alone occupies area which ranges between one-third to three-fifths of the cropped area during these years. The area under sugarcane, which is another important crop, has persistently dwindled from 10.7 per cent in 1968 to 6.9 per cent in 1985. It is quite surprising that the area under this crop has registered a steep decline though there is a sugar mill at Rohtak, a nearby city. Jowar is another important crop which is not raised as food crop but as fodder for the animals. Jowar (green and dry) in fact is the main source of fodder for the village.

Food Versus Non-Food Crops : Evidently, land use is heavily biased towards food crops which, among themselves, are grown to the extent of 75 per cent of the cropped area as in the year 1985. The sown area under food crops has registered an increase over the time period. But it is noticed that there are not many varieties among food crops. The increase in area under food-crops can singularly be explained with the spectacular increase in area under wheat. The area under wheat which was only 218 hectares in 1968 now stands at 389 hectares in 1985. The tremendous increase in area under wheat was due to the introduction and availability of high yielding variety seed of wheat. It may be noticed that area in respect of all other food crops like barley, gram and rice has declined considerably during the corresponding period. The fall in area under gram from 46 hectares in 1968 to a mere 3 hectares in 1983 is a matter of great concern as gram provided necessary nutrient to the villagers and the animals both. The decline in area under gram is largely due to waterlogging and the expanding land salinity.

The area under non-food crops fell from 29.2 per cent in 1968 to 11.8 per cent in 1985. There is not even a single crop from this group which showed any increase, instead these all shrunk in area during this period. Fodder has gained in area all through these years excepting 1985.

On the basis of the foregoing analysis of the cropping pattern some important conclusions can be drawn :

First, predominance of foodgrains together with the almost non-existence fruit and vegetable crops and the declining share of gram and sugarcane, the cropping pattern reflects the poor health of the people for whom the sources of physical nutrients such as calorie and protein are only cereals, pulses and sugar. Second, the picture of cropping pattern that is obtained in the village is a frozen one with a few insignificant changes except wheat. Some crops like sarson, vegetables, toria, remain inconspicuous in the cropping plan. Wheat at present, takes the lion's share of the cropped area as it did earlier. It has expanded tremendously by squeezing the land under gram, barley, sugarcane and traditional wheat. Third, the declining share of sugarcane, a cash crop, is a very serious matter which must be investigated fully. It was found during the course of discussion with the farmers that decline in area under sugarcane was largely because of the unremunerative procurement price of sugarcane fixed by the government. Farmers are also angry and against the coercive methods generally used by the government in procuring sugarcane to feed the Sugar Cooperative Mills at Rohtak.

The cropping pattern in the village is an outcome of many varied factors. The important factors being unsatisfactorily level of prices and rates, government policies and which have run counter to the farmers at different points of times. Factors relevant to soil and climatic conditions also have condtioned the cropping pattern in the village. All these factors have influenced the cropping pattern in the village in one way or the other. It is not possible to go into the details of these factors in analysing the cropping pattern because an exercise of this type is beyond the scope of this study.

However, some other important elements of cropping pattern like intensity of cropping, adopting of high-yielding variety seeds and the magnitude of crop wastage due to climatic and other hazards, are attempted here briefly.

Intensity of Cropping : We have already seen that the scope on extensive margin on land is quite limited. It is through intensity* of cropping only that land as a resource can be augmented. Intensity of cropping has increased over the time period barring the year 1985. Intensity of cropping which was 128 in 1968 rose to 170 in 1983. Now, little land is left as fallow and most of the land is double cropped. The land which remains fallow is due to multiplocity of reasons, absence or inadequate irrigation facility being the main reason. Unirrigated land is not suitable for double cropping. Besides, the owner of the land may simply be not prudent and not aware of the optimum land use and its cropping intensity. This may be owing to the farmer's traditional-bound ignorance to allow a fallow period for the land for sound crop rotation. For instance, most of the land put under wheat a Rabi crop, is that land which was kept reserved as fallow during the Kharif season. This practice is being followed by the numerous farmers in the village.

High Yieiding Varieties : The area brought under High Yielding Varieties (HYV) of seeds in food crops (wheat, rice and bajra) works out to be 92 per cent of the total cropped area under these crops in the village. Crop-wise, adoption of HYV in wheat, rice and bajra account for 95 per cent, 80 per cent and 70 per cent respectively. It may be seen that HYV, with the exception of bajra, are generally practised on the irrigated portion of the holding. The unirrigated component of holding remains in a disadvantageous position in process of securng the benefits of modern technological break-through in methods of growing high yielding variety crops. It is also proved that big farmers are relatively more active and move quickly in adopting the new varieties of crops. The reason for this would seem to lie in their relatively stronger resource base which makes them capable of procuring the necessary complementary supporting inputs such as cash, fertilisers,

---

$$\text{*Intensity of cropping} = \frac{\text{Area sown more than once x 100}}{\text{Sown area i.e. Cul tivated area}}$$

insecticides and irrigation. It is quite easy to infer that benefits from HYV programme, which was launched in the year 1968, are not being reaped equally by all categories of farmers. Hence, there is a great need for programme to design specifically to help the small farmers in adopting modern technology and thus partaking of the fruits of technological development of agriculture.

Crop Wasted

There occurs a serious and colossal damage and wastage of crops due to the natural hazards and other factors. The damage occurs at all stages from seedlings to harvesting and threshing. The loss due to crop wastage sometimes is considerable. For instance, the extent of crop loss in the village exceeded 27.3 and 26.5 per cent of the cropped area in 1978 and 1983 respectively. In case of individual crop, the loss sometimes is cent per cent. On the basis of the information supplied by the village Patwari, it came to light that bajra, an important Kharif crop, was completely destroyed by floods in three consecutive years from 1976 to 1978. Similarly, gram and wheat-gram mix, the two important Rabi crops, were totally damaged by some undetected disease in 1968. At times, farmers are even forced to reap the unripe crop because of hostile weather forecast. More recently, at the time of writing this report, nearly 25 per cent of the harvested wheat was damaged by an unprecedented hailstorm and bad stormy weather on the threshing floor itself. The hails weighing upto 400 gram lashed the region on the first day of May 1987. Indeed, vagaries of weather have played havoc with crops resulting in tremendous losses to peasants.

Certainly, farmers do suffer greatly on account of these natural hazards which are beyond their control. Considering that the farmers had invested sufficiently in the purchase of seed, chemical fertilizers, electricity, weedicides and mechanical as well as manual labour, the failure of crops proves a back-breaking experience for them. In view of the above adverse circumstances loaded against the farmers, the case for crop insurance would prove an important measure in providing increased agricultural investment and production and also in stabilizing agriculture. No sustained and steady development of the agriculture economy of the village is possible without some form of crop insurance to underwrite the risks of crop failure. The state government should give a serious thought to the possibility of introducing crop insurance on a larger scale. By doing so, the government can protect the farmers against the progressively rising costs of agricultural investment and the inherent risk in agriculture.

III

In this section, we briefly sketch the three important economic issues, namely, ownership of assets, occupational pattern and borrowing position in the village.

Ownership of Assets

For the purpose of analysis, all the assets have been classified into three categories viz (a) Household durables (b) Farm implements, and (c) Livestock. Let us analyse these factors individually.

(a) *Household Durables*: Tables 3.10(a) and 3.10(b) showed the ownership of a number of important household durables by members of various castes. It is observed that the ownership of consumer durables which reflects the standard of living of the people in the village is quite wide-spread. Regarding the availability of some luxurious durables in the village, our analysis confirms the common sense view of the social scientists that the durables like scooters, fans, televisions, sofa-sets, are concentrated in the hands of a few well-to-do families in the village. Their share in these assets is many times larger than their share in total number of households. It is not surprising, therefore, that the ownership of these durable items is concentrated among higher castes such as Brahmins and Jats. Further details, caste-wise and item-wise in respect of durables would throw more light on distributional aspect.

A wrist watch which was considered to be very conspicuous durable item in the past is now possessed by as many as 76.3 per cent of the families in the village. The quality of watch reflected in term of value, however, differs greatly among

TABLE 3.10 (a)

Availability of Households Durables

Caste	Watch		Cycle		Scooter	
	House-holds	Value (Rs.)	House-holds	Value (Rs,)	House-holds	Value (Rs.)
Ahir	—	—	—	—	—	—
Brahmin	24	523	20	366	1	6000
Jat	132	461	82	373	3	8000
Saini	28	529	27	347	1	8000
Baniya	—	—	1	400	—	—
Punjabi	—	—	1	350	—	—
Khati	5	650	4	525	—	—
Kumhar	1	300	3	550	—	—
Lohar	—	—	3	408	—	—
Nai	3	280	2	375	—	—
Sonar	3	500	3	416	—	—
Bairagi	6	430	5	420	—	—
Ḍoom	7	314	4	310	—	—
Chamar	40	261	44	350	—	—
Balmiki	34	260	17	349	—	—
Total/weighted average	283	418	216	369	5	7600
Percentage	76.3	—	58.2	—	1.3	—

Table 3.10 (a) *Contd.*

Caste	Sewing-Machine		Radio-set		T.V. Set		Tape-Recorder	
	House-holds	Value (Rs.)	House-holds	Value (Rs.)	House-holds	Value (Rs.)	Hous-holds	Value (Rs.)
Ahir	1	200	1	300	—	—	—	—
Brahman	13	339	23	244	2	2750	3	366
Jat	88	300	92	263	—	—	9	377
Saini	18	433	23	300	—	—	1	1000
Baniya	—	—	—	—	—	—	—	—
Puniabi	—	—	—	—	—	—	—	—
Khati	4	387	4	325	—	—	—	—
Kumhar	1	300	—	—	—	—	—	—
Lohar	1	350	1	270	—	—	—	—
Nai	3	330	1	300	—	—	1	600
Sonar	2	300	3	230	—	—	—	—
Bairagi	2	225	4	238	—	—	—	—
Doom	1	200	2	225	—	—	—	—
Chamar	9	242	25	255	—	—	6	312
Balmiki	6	240	19	254	—	—	4	310
Total/weighted average	149	314	198	234	2	2750	24	383
Percentage	40.2	—	53.4	—	0,5	—	6.5	

TABLE 3.10 (b)

Availability of Households Durables

Caste	Sofa-set		Table		Chair	
	House-holds	Value (Rs.)	House-holds	Value (Rs.)	House-holds	Value (Rs.)
Ahir	—	—	—	—	—	—
Brahmin	1	400	16	98	16	171
Jat	4	350	87	103	86	161
Saini	1	500	20	119	20	170
Baniya	—	—	—	—	—	—
Punjabi	—	—	—	—	—	—
Khati	—	—	4	80	4	148
Kumhar	—	—	—	—	—	—
Lohar	—	—	—	—	2	200
Nai	—	—	1	50	1	100
Sonar	—	—	2	100	—	—
Bairagi	—	—	4	62	4	106
Doom	—	—	—	—	—	—
Chamar	—	—	15	44	15	80
Balmiki	—	—	5	40	10	82
Total/weight average	6	383	154	95	158	148
Percentage	1.6	—	41.05	—	42.6	—

Table 3.10 (b) (*Contd.*)

Caste	Cot		Fan		Utensils	
	Households	Value (Rs.)	Households	Value (Rs.)	Households	Value (Rs.)
Ahir	3	55	1	250	3	127
Brahmin	31	85	14	430	29	447
Jat	153	66	89	561	150	384
Saini	33	56	14	538	30	454
Baniya	1	65	1	300	—	—
Punjabi	1	70	—	—	—	—
Khati	8	90	1	300	7	295
Kumhar	7	60	—	—	—	—
Lohar	13	75	1	300	5	308
Nai	3	80	1	525	3	316
Sonar	3	102	2	525	3	620
Bairagi	7	65	1	550	—	—
Doom	13	55	1	400	—	—
Chamar	45	58	5	300	50	150
Baimiki	50	55	3	250	43	110
Total/weight average	871	60	134	279	323	320
Percentage	100.00	—	36.1	—	87.1	

Table 3.10 (b) *Contd.*

Caste	Suitcase		Dress		Shoes	
	Hous holds	Value (Rs.)	House-holds	Value (Rs.)	House-holds	Value (Rs.)
Ahir	—	—	3	566	3	373
Brahmin	15	700	31	1241	31	319
Jat	107	822	153	1326	153	385
Saini	20	902	33	1106	33	349
Baniya	1	1236	1	2000	1	310
Punjabi	—	—	1	1000	1	200
Khati	4	375	8	1560	8	285
Kumhar	—	—	7	700	7	185
Lohar	4	263	13	1180	13	310
Nai	3	300	3	1216	3	267
Sonar	3	1133	3	533	3	400
Bairagi	7	414	7	560	7	254
Doom	3	83	13	401	13	226
Chamar	20	120	45	330	45	180
Balmiki	10	110	50	315	50	160
Total/weight						
Average	197	291	371	721	371	303
Percentage	53.1	—	100.0	—	100.0	

Note : (i) Value is the average market value per unit of an item per households in terms of rupees at the time of survey.

(ii) Percentages of households reporting an item in relation to total households.

castes. As expected, the value per watch is the lowest in case of Scheduled Caste families meaning thereby that they wear inferior quality watches. Cycle, another important household durable like watch, is also owned by a majority of families of all castes. Cycle which is used as a major mode of transportation by the villagers is possessed by 58.2 per cent households. The average value of cycle works out to be Rs. 369, although there are variations around this average among castes. Scooters have not yet invaded the village as these have done in the cities. There are only 5 scooters in the entire village – three owned by Jats and the remaining two by Brahmin and Saini one each. Scooter in the village is a status symbol. Sewing machine has also become quite popular and is owned by 40.2 per cent families almost from all the castes. It may, however, be noted that most of the sewing machines are used to repair and stitch clothes of the members of the households and not for earning. Many young girls who have discontinued their studies would like, in the first instant, to have sewing machines. The impressive number of sewing machines available in the village is also attributed to the dowry, as a sewing mechine has become a very common item for dowry these days. But it was also observed that most of the sewing machines thus given and obtained in dowry remain under-used and even completely unused in some cases and are reduced to junk in due course of time. The radio set has also become a common household acquisition. It is owned by more than 50 per cent of the families in the village. It is interesting to note that radio is equally popular among the Scheduled Castes where more than half of the families own it. It again, however, is a different matter that the radio-sets owned by Scheduled Castes families are of low quality as is evident from the value of radio-sets in Table 3.10 (a).

There are only two Brahmin families who possess television sets. A taste for tape-recorder, which was barely discernible about 10 years back, now seems to have caught on. It is also quite popular among the Scheduled Caste families as is evidenced by the number of tape-recorders possessed by members of these castes. The tape-recorder, as reported by the households, costs anything between Rs. 310 to Rs. 1000. Regarding items of furniture, it was noticed that these exist in proportions higher among much of the upper caste families as Brahmin, Jat and Saini. For instance, all the four sofa-sets in the village belonged to these castes. In case of fans, utensils (made of stainless steel), suitcases and dresses these castes again are placed in an advantageous position not only in terms of quantity but also in terms of quality. Other backward and Scheduled Castes are characterised by poor asset values. It may be surmised from the above analysis that the facilities of durable items mentioned above are enjoyed disproportionately more by upper castes families, but these items are also catching the fancy of many backward and Scheduled Castes families in the village.

(b) *Farm Implements* : Farm implements play a pivotal role in increasing agricultural production. To put it in other words, extensive use of farm machinery leading to mechanisation is indispensable for the growth of progressive agriculture. By mechanisation of agriculture we mean the replacement of animal and human power by machinery and as such ploughing is to be done by tractor, sowing and application of fertilizer by drill and harvesting and threshing by the combined harvester and so on.

Let us now examine the level of mechanisation of agriculture in terms of the availability and use of farm implements in the village. Each agriculture in the village has a minimum of agricultural tools and equipments of his own. It is, in fact, largely in the adoption of improved tools that one can see a change which may gradually influence the farmer's relations with the labours and their mode of employment. Not only this, the adoption of new types of agricultural implements is going to affect the farmer's relations with the village artisans and craftsmen. The factory-produced agricultural implements tend to render the local carpenter in obsolescence in the village.

It becomes clear on the basis of the information thrown by village survey that the cultivators in the village evince interest in new and improved kind of implements. For instance, there are 28 tractors in the village at present. The number of tractors owned by Jats is disproportionately large. Generally, big farmers having large size of land-holdings are able to maintain tractors. But it does not mean that tractors are owned exclusively by big farmers. There are also six small and medium farmers who maintain tractors. Interestingly, a Lohar with only a toy sized holding of one-fourth hectare also maintains tractor. The decision to buy tractor primarily is governed by the size of holding but it does also depend on such other factors as technical knowledge and strong inclination to have it. There are 34 farmers who have bored tubewells on their farms and these are mostly run with diesel engines. Khati, Ahir and Lohar who are engaged in cultivation do not have any tubewell. The number of wheat threshers in the village is 36 and these are largely owned by Jats. There are 63 bullock carts fitted with iron wheels. It is a common experience in the village that family not owning a cart, borrows it from the fellow cultivator. 'Buggi' a type of cart fitted with rubber tyres and drawn by single he-buffalo is replacing old style cart quite rapidly in the village. Number of iron ploughs is much less than the wooden ploughs. The wooden ploughs are locally made by the village carpenter and are cheaper than the iron ones. But steel plough is more useful and can be yoked to the iron plough. There are two crushers (*Kohlu*) in the village besides one power driven sugarcane crusher which comes in operation during the crushing season. The sugarcane crushers are often hired jointly by farmers for Rs. 500 from the stockists at Rohtak for the season. In addition, there are ten flour mills, one oil crusher and certain other implements whose statistics have been displayed in Tables 3.11 (a) and 3.11 (b).

(c) *Livestock* : The importance of cattle and other animals in Ladhot as in any other Haryanvi village can hardly be emphasized. The villagers, to a great extent, depend on animals which influence their day-to-day life. Milch cattle such as buffalos and cows are kept for milk and butter. Draft animals, like bullocks and he-buffalos, are kept for their usefulness for ploughing, lifting loads and pulling carts. Animal dung is used as manure and fuel. One can see everywhere piles of dung cakes prepared by the women-folk. It is a common sight in the village to the outside visitors. Cow-dung manure is far more superior and less expensive to modern chemical fert-

TABLE 3.11 (a)

Distribution of Farm Implements

(Number)

Caste	Cultivator	Farm-House	Tractor	Well	Tubewell
Ahir	1	1	—	—	—
Brahmin	29	2	3	—	4
Jat	152	8	23	3	28
Saini	29	—	1	—	1
Khati	1	—	—	—	—
Lohar	1	—	1	—	1
Total	213	11	28	3	34

Table 3.11 (a) *Contd.*

Caste	Harvester	Thresher	Disc Harrow	Cultivators	Seed Drill
Ahir	—	—	—	—	—
Branmin	—	5	3	3	2
Jat	1	28	23	10	14
Saini	—	3	2	2	2
Khati	—	—	—	—	—
Lohar	—	—	1	—	—
Total	1	36	29	15	18

TABLE 3.11 (b)

Distribution of Farm Implements

(Number)

Caste	Cart	Plough (Wooden)	Plough (Iron)	Sprayer	Duster
Ahir	1	1	—	—	—
Brahmin	6	3	—	—	—
Jat	46	54	18	—	—
Saini	10	11	—	—	—
Khati	—	—	—	—	—
Lohar	—	—	—	—	—
Total	63	69	18	—	—

Table 3.11(b) *Contd*

Caste	Flour Mill	Oil Crusher	Cattle-Shed	Implement Shed	Diesel Engine	Trolley
Ahir	—	—	—	—	—	—
Brahmin	—	—	—	—	5	3
Jat	9	—	19	9	34	5
Saini	1	1	—	—	—	1
Khati	—	—	—	—	—	—
Lohar	—	—	—	—	—	—
Total	10	1	19	9	39	9

ilizers. Livestock also provide subsidiary occupation and help in generating income particularly to the landless and marginal farmers.

The position of Ladhot village in the matter of animals can be gauged from Table 3.12. It is seen that there are varied types of animals in the village kept for different purposes. Among the milch cattle, buffalo is more popular than cow. Cows are kept only by about 16 per cent of the households as against 72 per cent who own buffalos. Not only this, the number of buflalos per household is 2.0 against 1.1 cow. Villagers prefer buffalo because of high yields of milk which is also rich in fats. A villager will go in for a cow only when buffalo is beyond his means. Some households maintain cow just for religious sentiments. Our analysis, however, strongly indicates that landless families who do not possess milch cattle in a large number deserve special assistance to enable them to own such animals for earning their livelihood.

Draft animals, understandably, are reported only from those families which are engaged in cultivation. Draft animals in the village are bullocks, he-buffalos and camels. However, the number of bullocks is much bigger in comparison with such other draft animals as he-buffalos and camels. The bullocks have been reported by 60 households and the number of bullocks per household is 1.5. It is interesting to note that many cultivators do not own any bullock or even other working animal. A cultivator, particularly the small one, can keep a pair of bullocks with great difficulty. Consequently, many such farmers hire tractor and also bullocks for doing agricultural operations on their land in different seasons. However, the system of hiring of bullocks in the village is quite uncommon. There are only three/four small farmers who are engaged in this practice. Small farmers also enter into some sort of a 'yoking' system of sharing their working cattle (and carts) with other farmers. But this practice is also not much in vogue these days and is dying out very rapidly.

It may be mentioned that he-buffalos are not preferred by the farmers for ploughing purposes as they are very slow, unsuitable and inferior to bullocks. All the same, it has become very popular because it has proved very useful in carting the

TABLE 3.12

Ownership of Animals and Cattle by Caste

Caste	Cow		Buffalos		Bullock		Young-Stock	
	Household	Percentage Average Household	Household	Percentage Average Household	Household	Percentage Average Household	Household	Percentage Average Household
Ahir	—	—	2	2.0	1	2.0	2	1.5
Brahmin	6	1.0	25	1.7	8	1.6	26	1.7
Jat	31	1.2	140	2.1	40	1.8	130	2.1
Saini	7	1.4	25	1.6	9	1.6	19	1.4
Baniya	—	—	—	—	—	—	—	—
Punjabi	—	—	—	—	—	—	—	—
Khati	1	1.0	5	2.5	1	1.0	3	1.3
Kumhar	—	—	1	1.0	—	—	1	1.0
Lohar	1	1.0	4	5.5	1	1.0	4	5.5
Nai	1	1,0	3.	1.0	—	—	3	2.3
Sonar	1	1.0	2	2.5	—	—	2	1.5
Bairagi	—	—	3	1.0	—	—	4	1.5
Doom	—	—	7	1.0	—	—	3	1.3
Chamar	7	1.4	29	1.6	—	—	30	1.7
Balmiki	4	1.4	20	1.6	—	—	21	1.7
Total	59	—	266	—	60	—	248	—
Average	—	1.1	—	2.0	—	1.5	—	1.9
Percentage	15.9	—	71.7	—	16.2	—	66.8	—

buggi Currently, there are about 50 he-buffalos in this village which are used for the purpose. The cost of upkeep of a he-buffalo is much lower than that of a bullock and hence economical. It has become quite difficult for an average farmer to maintain some good quality pair of bullocks especially in view of the non-availability of gram which is a must for their sustenance. The dwindling number of bullocks on farms is also attributed to the easy hiring facility of tractors. At the time of conducting this survey, no family reported use of camel. But some camels are brought by the farmers during winter season for cane crushing and are sold immediately after the season is over. Camels are not kept throughout the year. Camel in the village is not used for ploughing as is done in southern part of the state. The land in the village is dry, hard and grassy and thus camel ploughing is not feasible.

Besides the animals described above, there is another mixed category of animals in the village. These include pigs, sheep, poultry, birds and others. Only nine families, all belonging to Scheduled Castes, reported pigs and the number of pigs per household worked out 6.5. Pigs are a nuisance in the village. Complaints of trespassing are frequently heard against the pigs and this sometimes leads to quarrels. Despite all this, every villager recognises the services rendered by the pig in cleaning streets and open spaces on the borders of the village used as community latrines. Sheep numbering 122 only are kept by 17 Scheduled Caste households. Similarly, 24 goats in number are kept by Scheduled Caste families. There is only one family in the entire village which reported 5 poultry birds. There are some donkeys owned by Kumhars and only one horse was reported being kept by a Jat family in the village.

Animals in the village are not allowed to stray about. The only animals who are allowed to wander unhindered in fields are one adopted bull and two he-buffalos which are available for mating village cows and buffalos respectively.

It is significant to note that animals are treated with consideration and kindness. Both milch and working animals are treated as members of the household. The baby-calf is petted and loved by children and elders alike. In some orthodox families in the village, the first bread of the day is always fed to the cow. To feed properly and dust and bathe their animals is considered one of the serious duties of the farmers. Cows and buffalos that stop milching are never treated with cruelty. Same is the case with old bullocks. Animals are bedecked with garlands made of beautiful feathers of peacock on the eve of Divali festival.

Occupational Pattern

The occupational pattern vastly determines and reflects the distribution of households according to different occupations. It is an undisputed fact that there is a close relationship between development of an economy and occupational structure. The level of economic development gets accelerated with the shifting of abundant labour force from agriculture to industries and services. The Planning Commission in India has also realised the need to affect a change in the occupational structure through a transfer of a part of the labour force from agriculture to secondary and tertiary activities. A major objective of five year plans has also been to mobilize, to the maximum extent, the abundant labour force in the country for purposes of quick economic development. In the light of the above it would be of interest to consider the evidence of occupational changes in the village. Table 3.13 indicates changes in the occupational pattern in the village over the time period.

It is interesting to make comparison of the census figures in respect of occupational structure of the village. Though the definition of 'worker' in the different censuses has not been uniform, yet some conclusions can be drawn. The occupational structure reflects a clearly heavy bias towards agr'cultural activities. Over the past twenty years, the proportion of working population engaged in primary sector, agriculture and allied activities has not fallen below 63 per cent. This is a clear indication of the prevalence of large scale disguised unemployment in agriculture in the village. The proportion of working force in the secondary and tertiary sectors has been almost steady during this period. A very important factor which has hindered the change in occupational structure since 1961 is the relatively high ratio of growth of labour force consequent

TABLE 3.13

Occupational Structure Since 1961

(Number)

	1961			1971			1981		
	Male	Female	Total	Male	Female	Total	Male	Female	Total
Cultivators	261	259	520	261	4	265	276	170	446
Agricultural Labour	94	84	178	73	—	73	96	7	103
Manufacturing and Construction	30	1	31	22	2	24	—	—	—
Trade and Transport	5	—	5	7	—	7	80	4	84
Other Services	13	—	13	45	2	47	—	—	—
Total Workers	403	344	747	408	8	416	452	181	633

Source : Census reports.

upon the rapidly increasing population. The only way to change the occupational structure is to foster the growth of non-agricultural employment in the village.

Now, we examine the occupational distribution among castes. Generally, occupation in any village is closely related to caste. Each caste has a specific occupation which is more or less predetermined and one is expected to practise that on adulthood. For instance, a carpenter's son will be engaged in house-building activities and construction of agricultural implements which cater to the needs of the farmers. A Goldsmith will prepare ornaments for the villagers. Similarly, kumhars and blacksmiths take to pitcher making and smithy respectively. In this manner, every caste is mostly conditioned by tradition to a specific position in the structure of the village community and a definite economic function which is heir main source of living.

In order to make our analysis simple and meaningful, occupation is studied under three broad categories-traditional, sole and subsidiary. Traditional occupation is defined as one determined for each caste which constitutes an occupational group. Sole occupation means the only occupation which is followed by the household. It may be either traditional occupation or otherwise. Subsidiary occupation means the occupation which is supplementary to the traditional occupation. It may happen that if the traditional occupation is not quite rewarding and fails to meet the minimum requirements of the household, then it may either be given up altogether and substituted by another occupation or supplemented by some subsidiary occupation. Table 3.14 presents the distribution of families according to this classification of occupations.

An examination of Table 3.14 reveals that out of 371 families in the village as many as 266 families (71.7 per cent followed only one occupation and the rest 105 families had taken to some subsidiary occupation. It is noticed that agriculture was practised by 123 families (33.9 per cent) as the sole occupation. 60 families (16.2 per cent) worked as sole casual labourers, and 188 families (50.6 per cent) followed non-agricultural occupations like business, teaching, defence, tailoring, etc. It is quite evident that the bulk of population which is land l

TABLE 3.14

Distribution of Households Following Different Occupation in the Village

Caste	Traditional Occupation	Sole Occupation		Subsidiary Occupation		Total
Ahir	Agriculture	Agriculture	2	—		3
		Labour	1			
Brahmin	Priest and Service	Agriculture	14	Service	9	
		Service	4	Shopkeeper	2	31
				Milkvender	1	
				Labour	1	
Jat	Agriculture	Agriculture	90	Service	38	
		Service	8	Flour Mill	2	
				Cane-Crusher	1	
				Milk-Selling	4	153
				Transport (Tempo)	1	
				Pension	5	
				Labour	2	
				Shopkeeper	2	
Saini	Agriculture	Agriculture	5	Service	9	
		Tailor	1			

1	2	3	4	5	6	7
		Labour	2	—	—	33
		Business	1			
		Service	5		—	1
Baniya	Shopkeeping	Shopkeeping	1	—	—	1
Punjabi	Shopkeeping	Shopkeeping	1	—	—	1
Khati	Carpentry	Carpentry	1			
		Agriculture	1	—	—	
		Wood-shop	1		—	8
		Labour	3			
		Service	2			
Kumhar	Pottery	Potter	5			
		Service	1	—	—	7
		Ojha	1			
Lohar	Blacksmithy	Agriculture	1	—		
		Dairy	1			
		Labour	4		—	13
		Shopkeeping	1			
		Driver	1			
		Families settled in city	5			

1	2	3	4	5	6	7
Nai	Hair-drcssing	Hair dressing	1	Labour plus	1	3
		Tea-shop	1	Ojha		
Sonar	Goldsmithy	Goldsmithy	1	—		3
		Service	2			
Bairagi	Labour and	Labour	4	—		
	Singing Song	Shopkeeper	1			7
		Service	2			
Doom	Entertainment	Entertainment	7	Labour	2	13
		Labour	2			
		Service	2			
Chamar	Shoe-making	Service	15			
	and Labour	Labour	20	Labour	10	45
Balmiki	Labour and	Labour	25	Service	13	50
	Sanitation	Service	10	Sanitation	2	
Total			266		105	3 71

worked as farm labourers since there was no other alternative occupation available to them in the village. It is also evident from the above analysis that agriculture constitutes the very core of the economic activities pursued in the village. In a large measure it is the main source of livelihood for the households. It is quite surprising that the artisans continued in their respective trades for long without any skill formation. They in fact require improved tools and equipment and marketing assistance to withstand the severe competition from organised industries. A caste-wise analysis would provide deep in-sight into it and would also determine the extent of dependence on traditional and non-traditional occupation of the households.

Among Ahirs, two out of three families followed agriculture which is their traditional occupation and one worked as labourer. The Brahmins, a priestly caste by traditions, have taken to agriculture and also did all other odd jobs like shopkeeping, milk vending, etc. One elderly Brahmin—a recognised freedom fighter, draws pension and lives along with his family in Rohtak. Most of the Jats (59 per cent) are engaged in agriculture—the traditional occupation of this caste. A large number of families from this caste are also engaged in other occupations including business, civil and military services. Those in service, are mosty in teaching and army. It is notable that all the three gazetted posts in the village are held by Jats-one is a major in the army, the other is a lecturer in Government College and the third a Sub-Inspector of Police in Delhi. Clearly, some occupational mobility among Jats is perceptible. However, Jats consider it degrading having to work as labour on others' farms. It is interesting to note that even the poorest of Jats do not hire out their services as manual labour in the village. In case of Sainis mobility in their traditional occupation has been noticed. They have started to undertake new occupations like tailoring and driving. There are nine Saini families whose subsidiary occupation is service. Baniya and Punjabi households have mostly stuck to their traditional occupations of shopkeeping. Owing to compelling circumstances the craftsmen such as Khati, Kumhar, Lohar and Sonar have largely switched over to varied types of non-traditional professions and activities. Out of the eight families of Khati caste, one is engaged in carpentry and the rest have taken to other such occupations as agriculture, labour and service. It is significant to note that all the families of Lohars are engaged in other occupations and have given up the traditional occupations altogether. Thus, there is complete switch-over of traditional profession in case of Lohars. Not only this, five Lohar families are permanently settled in cities as their craftsmen position in the village had become quite precarious. More or less, the same holds good about Nais and Sonars. Bairagi and Doom, like other castes, are also trying hard to switch over to other occupations to eke out their living. One person from the Doom caste is a non-commissioned officer (Subedar) in the army. Scheduled Castes are also no exception to the changing occupational pattern and they now tend to be absorbed largely in services and other avenues available to them within and outside the village. The village Chamars serve in the army and the police. Similarly, there are 16 men and young boys of Balmiki caste who are in active service in the Indian Army. Two Balmikis serve as village chowkidars. Two Balmiki families have migrated and settled in urban areas for their living. But many families of Scheduled Castes continue to remain absorbed, as indicated above, as landless lobourers or workers. From the foregoing analysis some following broad conclusions can be drawn.

First, agriculture is followed by many of the castes who own some land in the village. And agriculture is a common vocation without any caste barrier. Secondly, as the bulk of population is landless, it is but natural that such families work as labourers. Thus, the number of agricultural workers who depend on the cultivation of land is quite large in the village. Thirdly, the interdependence of castes as reflected in terms of specification of occupation is breaking down. This is largely happening due to the monetization of rural sector where both the parties prefer to do a service for cash payment. Apart from this, the new methods of doing things and new technology has also ushered in an altogether different relationship between the patron and the client. Fourthly, the number of families of service-holders and other vocations is quite encouraging. And the tendency of the people towards caste occupation is dwindling and the fact of caste identification with the traditional occupation remains somewhat less identified. Some new occupations have been added to the traditional pattern. Several castes are trying to have new occupations. Fifthly, though families are trying to adopt new occupations but have not shown much potential keeping in view the favourable location of the village which is hardly eight kilometers from the Rohtak city. Sixthly, econmic development of the village will necessarily have to involve a transfer of at least a part of the working force from agriculture to non-agricultural activities. Currently migration from the village to the city has taken place from a cross-section of the population but it tends to be more strong among the more intelligent, the educated and the well to-do. And as this movement steadily continues, the village population tends to become more sodden, less virile and more inert. Lastly, it is revealed that most of the families, particularly the small farmers are not satisfied with their present occupation. Most of them want their children to join such of the other professions as industry, business or some white-collar government jobs. The families satisfied with their present occupation are mostly those having some other subsidiary source of income.

Workers and Non-Workers

The work force is the single important indicator in the measurement of economic activity. The work force participation rate depends upon such factors as age, sex-composition, attitude to work and availability of work etc. The work participation rate in the village according to 1981 census is 27 per cent whereas similar figures for 1961 and 1971 were 50 per cent and 22 per cent respectively. Table 3.15 reveals that work force participation ratio has declined from 50 per cent in 1961 to 27 per cent in 1981.

It should, however, be kept in mind that the above figures are not strictly comparable because the concept of 'worker' or labour force has been changing from census to census. During 1961 census, many such workers whose main activity was not economic were classified as workers. Thus, many housewives and students were treated as workers in 1961 census.

TABLE 3.15

Working and Non-Working Population

	1961			1971			1981		
	Male	Female	Total	Male	Female	Total	Male	Female	Total
Workers	403	344	747	408	8	416	452	181	633
Marginal Workers	—	—	—	—	—	—	31	20	51
Non-workers	374	375	749	559	917	1476	701	832	1533
Total	777	719	1496	967	925	1892	1184	1033	2217

This obviously resulted in the exaggeration of the work force participation rate. A worker, according to 1971 census, is a person whose main activity is to participate in any economically productive work by his/her physical or mental activity. It may also be emphasised that the census of 1981 carried forward the tradition of the census of 1971 in making the definition of 'worker' rigorous and more meaningful, and comprehensive and has classified the workers into main 'worker' and 'marginal worker. Main workers are those who have worked in some economic activity over a period of six months or more and marginal workers are those who have not worked for a major part of the year. But the fact remains that proportion of unproductive population is quite substantial. Regarding the work participation ratio between the sexes evidently is much less in case of females as compared with their male counterparts.

Non-Workers and Unemployment

The incidence of unemployment in the village is very heavy. The total village population of non-workers accounts for 70 per cent. There is prevalence of chronic under-employment or disguised unemployment and also unemployment among the educated young persons. In fact, the unemployment in the village has two aspects—seasonal and perennial. For several months in a year during the slack season a sizeable portion of the population engaged in agriculture remains idle. This is a sort of situation where apparently every-one seems to be engaged in some or the other activity though enough work is not available to all. The scope of this study did not permit us to exactly measure this type of unemployment but rough estimates indicated that it is in no case less than 30 per cent. The implication is that nearly one-third working force engaged in agriculture can be removed without having any diminutive effect on agriculture. In other words, the marginal productivity of labour tends to become zero which implies that a large labour force can be dispensed with easily without adversely affecting agriculture in the village.

The second type of unemployment exists among the educaled persons. There are, at present, many educated youth who have failed to get any job. Several of them have spent a very long period of joblessness leading to frustration. The excessively long period of waiting has also told upon the physical and mental health of these young persons with the results that they have developed famished looks.

Another serious feature of unemployment in the village is that it is widely spread among poor families. The well-to-do, however, are able to manage jobs for the member of their families. Such families generally have political leverage and can also afford gratification required for getting a job. To secure even the lowest employment in army, police and other services a tidy sum is required which is beyond the means of poor people in the village.

Owing to serious unemployment situation, there is heavy discontentment among the village youths who constitute a potent threat to social stability. It is vitally necessary that unemployment particularly the educated unemployment, should be reduced to minimum. To relieve unemployment and under-employment in the village, a programme of rural industrialization should be launched. The feasibility of setting up the industries based on local characters such as cane-crushing, rice-shelling, processing of agriculture products may be tried seriously. The various programmes launched by the government have not been successful in alleviating poverty and removing unemployment because of the inherent weakness of these programmes. The recently much publicised programme of the State government such as giving unemployment doles to the unemployed and their free travel in Haryana buses for attending interviews for jobs are palliatives and are not the permanent solution of the problem in the long run. If the employment policy is to be of any success, then a vigorous and persistent population policy aiming at reducing birth rate should be implemented. Thus, the solution of unemployment lies in increasing the absorptive capacity of the village on the one hand and in the adoption of a positive population policy on the other.

Saving and Borrowing

Savings : A high rate of saving can pave the way for the

economic growth of the village. It is evident that the current rate of saving is very low. Table 3.16 portrays some details regarding the households who save and also the places where they keep their savings.

A glance at Table 3.16 will reveal that average saving* per household is Rs. 3540 although there are wide variations around this average. The highest saving (Rs. 6363) per family is among Jats and the lowest (Rs. 531) among the Lohars. It is worth mentioning that the savings of Chamars are much more than some of the non-Scheduled Castes like Nai, Sonar, Bairagi, Khati and Punjabi. An analysis of the break-up of the saving accounts sourcewise would reveal that of the total saving, 37.4 per cent is kept in the banks, 16.5 per cent in post offices, 9.8 per cent with L.I.C. and the remaining 36.3 per cent is kept at home. It is encouraging to note that banks attract savings and villagers are developing banking habits in the matter of handling their savings. It was further revealed that a significant proportion of cultivators kept their savings with banks and other financial institutions while Scheduled Castes, illiterates and labouring classes did not keep their savings with either a bank or the post offices.

Borrowing : In case of borrowings, the revealing feature stemming out of our survey is that most of the households in the village depend upon outside finance to meet their pressing financial requirements. Borrowing if utilized properly, is not necessarily objectionable, and nor a sign of weakness either. But when it is diverted for unproductive purposes such as celebration of marriages, births, deaths and for litigations then it works as the hangman's rope. Unproductive loans raised at exorbitant rates of interest are highly improper and unjustified. Table 3.17 summarises information regarding the number of households who depend on borrowing in the village.

Table 3.17 constructed on the basis of borrowers' interview shows that more than one-third households (36.7 per cent) are involved in the practice of borrowing. The amount of borrowing varies considerably between castes. In general, the upper

* There was a general tendency among the respondents to understate the saving, in the main, to the fear that the information thus given might make them subject to some sort of tax.

TABLE 3.16
Savings in the Village

Caste	Household Reporting Saving in Bank	Savings (Rs.)	Household Reporting Saving in P.O.	Savings (Rs.)	Household Reporting Saving in LIC
Ahir	—	—	—	—	—
Brahmin	6	37,350	7	21,000	5
Jat	40	3,70,850	37	1,74,750	19
Saini	3	12,000	6	6,500	1
Baniya	—	—	—	—	—
Punjabi	—	—	—	—	—
Khati	—	—	—	—	—
Kumhar	1	3,000	1	1,500	—
Lohar	—	—	—	—	—
Nai	1	10,000	—	—	—
Sonar	—	—	1	1,500	—
Bairagi	1	6,000	5	2,400	—
Doom	5	34,600	1	6,000	—
Chamar	4	10,000	1	3,000	—
Balmiki	2	7,000	—	—	—
Total Households	63	4,90,800	59	2,16,650	25
Averge Saving Pereentage to the Total Saving	—	37.4	—	16.5	—

(*Contd.*)

Caste	Savings (Rs.)	Household Reporting Saving at Home	Savings (Rs.)	Total Savings (Rs.)	Saving per Average Household
Ahir	—	3	4,200	4,200	1,400
Brahamin	13,700	18	29,000	1,01,050	3,260
Jat	1,10,000	112	3,18,020	9,73,620	6,363
Saini	5,000	18	30,750	54,250	1,644
Baniya	—	1	1,000	1,000	1,000
Punjabi	—	1	600	600	600
Khati	—	7	6,400	6,400	800
Kumhar	—	1	5,000	9,500	1,357
Lohar	—	6	6,900	6,900	531
Nai	—	2	900	10,900	3,633
Sonar	—	1	250	1,750	583
Bairagi	—	1	250	8,650	1,236
Doom	—	7	5,360	45,960	3,535
Chamar	—	40	40,000	53,000	1,178
Balmiki	—	45	28,640	35,640	713
Total Households/ In average Saving	1,28,700	263	4,77,270	13,13,42	3540
Percentage to the total saving	9.8	—	36.3		100

TABLE 3.17

Number of Borrowing Households from Different Sources

Caste	Money-lender	Friends	Co-op. Society	Land Development-Bank	Other Banks	Other Agency	Total
Ahir	—	—	—	1	—	—	1
Brahmin	3	3	—	8	2	2	18
Jat	10	17	—	30	9	5	71
Saini	3	—	—	11	2	4	20
Baniya	—	—	—	—	—	—	—
Punjabi	—	—	—	—	—	—	—
Khati	—	—	—	—	1	—	1
Kumhar	1	—	—	—	—	—	1
Lohar	—	—	—	—	1	—	1
Nai	—	—	—	—	1	—	1
Sonar	—	—	—	—	—	—	—
Bairagi	—	—	—	—	—	—	—
Doom	—	—	—	—	3	—	3
Chamar	3	5	—	—	—	4	12
Balmiki	2	3	—	—	—	2	7
Total	22	28	—	50	19	17	136
Percentage	16.2	20.6		36.7	14.0	12.5	100

castes owe more borrowings. The proportion of households who borrowed is the highest for Jats followed by Sainis and Brahmins—all the three agriculturist castes. It appears that borrowing has become, more or less, inevitable for them to carry out cultivation. Interestingly, Scheduled Castes did not resort to much of borrowing. And the belief that the lower castes are overburdened with debt is unfounded. Amongst the lower castes, debts are unusual and wherever they occur the source is usually the money-lenders.

The important sources of finance for the villagers are lenders, friends and relatives, the Land Development Bank, other banks and certain miscellaneous sources. The important source of credit in village is Land Mortgage Bank now called the Land Development Bank (LDB). The LDB which caters to the needs of the people of this area is situated at Rohtak. The percentage of households who have borrowed from this bank works out to be 36.7. We shall refer to this source somewhat in detail later. It is clear from Table 3.17 that 22 households in the village have borrowed from money-lenders. This figure appears to be based on underestimate as some other households might not have disclosed their debt position in relation to money-lenders. But it was definite that all these loans are from within the village and not from outside. In the village they come mostly from four or five households who combine money-lending with other activities.

Sometimes the landlord also provides loan to the tenant. Most of these loans are for one year but can possibly be raised and renewed at a high interest rate. The most usual interest rate for a private loan was 24 per cent. The rate is likely to be higher where the loan was for consumption, where a marriage was being financed, or where the borrower was a member of Scheduled Caste. An indepth analysis would reveal that borrowing made by cultivators from money-lenders is generally not utilized for the purchase of agricultural inputs. Conversely, farmers think of some other government institutions as the right place to secure credit for those purposes. The incidence of borrowing from relatives and friends is only 20.6 per cent. This type of borrowing is generally affected in order to tide over temporary difficulties. These loans are contracted in an informal manner, they carry low or no interest and normally these are returned soon. But since this source of finance is uncertain, households do not depend upon this to any larger extent, and the importance of this source, these hard-days is on the decline.

Turning to institutional finance, it may be stated that the need for such a finance arises because of the weakness or inadequacy of private agencies to supply finance at reasonable rates of interest and with other easy conditions. Institutional credit is never exploitative as the basic motive three is always to help the borrower to raise his productivity and maximise his income. The rate of interest is relatively low and still lower for some specific purposes. Table 3.17 notes that the percentage of households who borrowed finance from cooperatives, LDB, banks and other agencies are zero, 36.8 per cent, 13.8 per cent and 12.5 per cent respectively. As mentioned earlier in Chapter 2, the Co-operative society in the village which functioned for sometimes was wound up on account of its malfunctioning.

As promised earlier, let us now complete our description of the borrowing from LDB. Importantly, the finance advanced by this bank figures conspicuously in the over all financial structure of the village. The need for long term loans of the farmers is looked after by this bank. Infact, to provide long-term credit to the cultivators against the mortgage of their lands is the major objective of this bank. The loans from the LDB are very cheap. The rate of interest varies between 4.5 per cent to 12.5 per cent and loans are spread over a long span of time, say, 5 to 10 years. The number of households in the village who availed of loan from the LDB is 50. Out of these, 38 are the small and medium farmers and the remaining 12 happen to be big farmers. Purposewise loan availed by farmers is given in Table 3.18.

A close peep into the table would reveal that small and medium farmers usually take loans more for the installation of tubewells than for any other purposes. The big farmers avail this loan mainly for the purchase of tractor. Small and medium farmers take loan also for the purpose of squaring up their old loan. Facts about big farmers are different. The

TABLE 3.18

Purposewise Loan Availed by Farmers From the LDB

Purpose of Loan	Small and Medium Farmer	Percentage of Total	Big Farmers	Percentage of Total
Tubewell	29	76.4	5	41.7
Tractor	1	2.6	6	50.0
Redemption of Loan	4	10.5	—	—
Diesel Engine	4	10.5	1	8.3
Total	38	100	12	100

next important item, for which loan from LDB is availed is the diesel engine which is put to multipurpose uses.

The total amount outstanding as loan from the LDB is quite substantial. It comes to Rs. 7,07,000 which works out at Rs. 14,140 per borrower. The rate of interest is 12.5 per cent or less which is lower in comparison with other traditional sources of finance. The period of loan, as indicated already, varies between 5 to 10 years and is repayable in easy instalments. For the enterprising farmer LDB has been an attractive source of loan. Infact, the loans from LDB have enabled Ladhot farmers to acquire tractors and tubewells in recent years. Many farmers stated that these loans have increased their productive capacity and impact of loans on the whole, has been favourable.

It may, however, be pointed out that farmers usually experience some difficulties in obtaining loans from LDB. The main difficulty is said to be the long time taken for the disbursement of this loan. This is particularly so in case of small farmers who are less influential. Repayment of loans to the bank is another constant source of worry to the farmers. Repayment period should be extended in case of emergency. As we know, try as we may, fields cannot become factory and crops are exposed to numerous natural hazards including disease, droughts, untimely rain, floods, winds and hail-storms. In the wake of any such unforeseen situation the bank should take a lenient view in the matter of recovery of loan.

From the above analysis, we are now in a position to review the overall incidence of borrowings amongst various castes in Ladhot. The overall borrowing position is somewhat significant. Jats are over-burdened with borrowed money. It is evident that some efforts seem to have been made to provide adequate alternative sources of credit to the villagers but many problems are associated with these types of finances which still persist. Poor families continue to be exploited by the money-lenders and landlords. There is dire need to restart the rural credit society which was abandoned after its poor performance in the village. This will help to provide more and instant credit at proper rates to meet the growing needs of the households of all castes. The two-pronged policy to curtail and regulate the activities of money-lenders and to expand the scope of institutional finances should be adhered to carefully and sincerely by the government.

CHAPTER 4

SOCIAL AND CULTURAL LIFE, POWER AND AUTHORITY INFLUENCE

In order to understand fully an Indian village, it is necessary to acquire knowledge regarding its social and cultural life and also the power and authority influence. There is a strong linkage between the status of an economy and these non-economic agents. The present chapter is an attempt to explore these salient socio-cultural and other characteristics of the village. The agents of change which have been selected are: house accommodation and settlement of houses, attitude towards education, nutrition and food, marriages, caste relations, habits and hobbies and functioning of the village Panchayat. The analysis opens out with a discussion on housing conditions in the village.

Housing Pattern

A brief description of the pattern of village houses and their arrangements has been made in Chapter 2. It is intended here to give more details of the living accommodations in terms of space, rooms and amenities.

There are some basic and distinct characteristics of houses that one could see in the village. The houses are in cluster in a compact area. The houses mostly are pucca and are made of bricks. There are only a few houses which arc kucha and made of mud. In many houses there is a boundary wall. The courtyard attached to these houses varies in size from tiny to the quite spacious, and in many cases, it is even bigger than the size of the main house itself. Cooking, generally, takes place in the courtyard. The entry to the courtyard is always by a door. Many rich families were found to have constructed small reception room (Poli, Baithak) immediately attached to the front door. This is an introduction of urban way of life and this arrangement is similar to that of a drawing room in city houses. But, it is found mostly in case of well-to-do families who are in service. This arrangement allows greater privacy to women folk of the households who do not need to be seen so frequently by the visitors. This form of construction is significant in view of the practice of veiling (Parda) system in the village. Under this system young girls and newly married women avoid being seen by strangers. It is to be noted in this context that a male stranger does not enter the family quarters of another unless special business brings him there. Then, he usually enters escorted by a man of the family, coughing loudly to suggest to the females to go into seclusion. Similarly, the instant an elderly man of the family enters the house, women in the house become self-conscious covering their faces, lowering their heads and in every way emphasising their sex and their role as subordinate.

We now focus our attention on Table 4.1 which gives varied types of information in respect of house accommodation.

There is ample evidence to show that villagers attach importance to good houses. Table 4.1 reveals that the number of residential houses is more than the number of households. And the average number of houses owned by a family in the village works out to be 1.3. Caste-wise position in this respect would further reveal that this average is the highest for Brahmins. Notably, there were only two families of Baniya and Punjabi in the entire village who do not possess houses of their own and reside in rented buildings. The solitary Punjabi family is paying building rent at the rate of Rs. 100 per month. Similarly, single Baniya family which has been living in this rented house for the last 10 years pays rent at the rate of Rs. 150 per month.

TABLE 4.1
Houses and Amenities at Ladhot

Caste	No. of Houses	Pucca	Kucha	No. of Houses per Family	Rooms per House	Kitchen per House	House Area in Meteres	Cattle-shed per Households
Ahir	4	4	—	1.3	5.0	0.6	280	1.0
Brahmin	56	55	1	1.8	5.5	0.8	252	1.0
Jat	230	227	3	1.5	5.3	0.6	240	1.3
Saini	43	43	—	1.3	5.2	0.5	220	1.0
Baniya	1	1	—	1.0	—	—	—	—
Punjabi	1	1	—	1.0	—	—	—	—
Khati	8	8	—	1.0	5.0	0.5	113	1.0
Nai	3	2	1	1.0	5.0	0.5	86	1.0
Kumhar	7	7	—	1.0	2.0	—	100	—
Lohar	18	16	2	1.4	4.0	0.5	200	0.5
Sonar	4	4	—	1.3	4.0	0.5	123	1.0
Bairagi	7	4	3	1.0	2.5	0.4	110	—
Doom	13	10	3	1.0	3.8	0.5	142	—
Chamar	45	36	9	1.0	3.0	0.4	110	—
Balmiki	50	34	16	1.0	2.2	0.3	96	—
Total/Weighted Average	490	452	38	—	—	—	—	0.5
Percentage	—	—	—	—	103	0.4	141	0.5

Note : Baniya and Punjabi who do not possess houses of their own reside in rented buildings in the village.

Houses, by and large, are *pucca*. There are only 38 houses which are *Kucha* and most of these belong to Scheduled Caste families. The material used in the construction of kucha houses consist of clay mixed with wheat straw. The walls as well as the top of the roof are plastered with mud. The door and window frames and shutters of the houses are wooden, made available from local market or from Rohtak city. A kucha house, even if maintained properly and repaired regularly, can last only for a limited number of years, say, 15 to 20 years. The kucha houses, which are quite limited in number, in the village are on their way out. And whenever a kucha house collapses or becomes dilapidated then invariably a pucca house is built in this place. And the result has been that a great deal of reconstruction of houses has taken place in the village in recent years.

Pucca houses are of varied types although no big efforts are generally made to follow the construction strictly on some set and concrete architectural planning. As already mentioned, now almost every family has the tendency to convert the house into a brick and mortar affair. The interior of many houses now gives different looks, and a colour wash on urban style is the craze with several households. It was also observed that villagers rarely construct their houses at one go, it is in phases. It was also noticed that roofs and floors of many pucca houses are kucha. The roofing is done in many cases with tiles, timbers and earth.

The average number of rooms per family comes to 3.6. But in case of Scheduled Castes it is much less. Many houses do not seem to be quite spacious as the average area covered is 141 metres only. This also gives some idea of the degree of pressure of population on housing accommodation in the village. The situation becomes worse when the family disintegrates and the house building is partitioned depending on the number of claimants. A very important feature of the houses which, at once, is noticeable is that very often the walls separating the houses are common and the houses do not seem to be quite separated. The above situation obtained in respect of the layout of houses, clearly reveals that the privacy in these houses is minimal. The inadequacy of privacy in these houses needs to be well remembered particularly when family planning methods are thought as a means to control the growing village population. Similarly, as the privacy between the houses is not possible to maintain, a quarrel among the members of the house can never remain a family affair but soon gets currency in the whole neighbourhood as the houses are chained together.

Even less than one-half of the households have any separate kitchen. Kitchen here means a room set apart for cooking and not for any other purpose. Castewise, the proportion of those having provision for separate kitchen, was the highest for Brahmins followed by Jats. Kitchen facilities, as expected, rank very poorly in case of Scheduled Caste families and cooking is done in the open. It is done on the traditional mud hearth using fire-wood and dung cakes. There are only two families in the village who use modern fuel (LPG) for cooking. It is noteworthy that stove/oven (*chulha*) is kept ceremonially clean, with a fresh coating of clay paste frequently. But the chief-drawback of this *chulha* is that it lacks a chimney and the smoke gushes into the face and eyes of the woman doing the cooking.

Attempts have been made in the village to devise a *chulha* which does not have the defects of traditional chulha. But there is hardly any smokeless chulha in the entire village. This chulha, which can be of several designs, has advantage over the old chulha. In this chulha smoke is emitted through chimney. It makes possible for the kettle of food to cook slowly or be kept warm at the back of the stove while some other item is being cooked over the flame at the front. On the ordinary chulha only one thing can be cooked at a time. The improved chulha was introduced by National Service Scheme (NSS) cadets who camped in the village in the year 1985. But to one surprise, it was discovered during the survey that women still cling to the old smoking chulha despite its drawbacks.

The position regarding separate bath-room in the house is quite worse. Bath-room here means a separate room used exclusively for bathing and washing purposes. Bath-room does not get any priority at the time of designing a house. Nearly 90 per cent male members, usually, take their bath in the open in the fields or in the courtyard of the house. Ladies experience great difficulty in taking bath due to the absence of proper bath-room facilities. They generally take bath under the cover of darkness at night or within the main house building during the day. Ladies who take bath during day time use improvised bath facilities. There are no proper toilet facilities in the village. The grown up people are always found in search of some blind corner in the street suitable for passing urine. Males go and ease themselves in nearby fields and ladies and children on the periphery of the village. This creates most unhygienic conditions in the village. There is no proper drainage system for discharge of used water with the result that it stagnates and stinks badly in the streets.

There are very few cattle sheds that are separate from the main residential buildings. Hardly, one-half of the households claim this facility. The households that do not have this facility keep and together their cattle in the residential building. Evidently, the situation where the human and the cattle share a common roof, is quite unnatural and unhygienic. It was also observed that those who possess cattle-sheds use these as a store for agricultural implements, perhaps, for want of space in the residential portion. Bullock carts in dismantled form, invariably, are hung on the sides of walls of the sheds.

There appear also compost pits near the habitation which are not properly kept. Cow-dung is used for making fuel cakes. But the urine passed by the cattle goes waste. All this waste goes to nearby ponds of the village where cattle drink water all the year round. This renders heads of cattle vulnerable to various kinds of disease.

Attitude Towards Education

A majority of people in the village is found to be conscious of the need for education and they give priority to it. However, they are unable to improve school education and the environment in general. In raising funds for the school, the villagers always evince great enthusiasm. This fact has already been mentioned in Chapter 2. Despite general awareness, people feel helpless in monitoring the quality of education in panted in the village schools. The teachers do not make sincere efforts to improve the effectiveness and the standard of education. It is an irony of circumstances that teachers who are the agents of change seem to have lost all zeal in the matter. Most of the teachers in the village schools are daily commuters who come from the neighbouring villages and Rohtak city and attend to their routine work. They do not come in close contact with the parents of the students receiving education in the school. This has perhaps made them unable to identify themselves with the villagers and their wards. The result has been that those who have high educational aspirations are compelled to send their children to schools at Rohtak. This means more expenses and added inconvenience.

Nutrition and Food

The level of nutrition determines the physical and mental growth of population. It also determines the life expectancy of the people. Before we produce statistical facts of the village on this aspect, it would be pertinent to make some observations of a general nature. There has been a rapid decline in the physical standard of the people in the village. This can be said of other Haryana village. Average villager now is not as tall and stoutly healthy as he used to be earlier. The decline may not be apparenty visible to the casual observer but it clearly shows up in such things as the selection tests for services like police and the army. In the village, many young boys desirous to join police or army do not meet the height and chest expansion requirements. The physical standard is definitely going down. Several factors could be attributed to this, but genetic make up and food are squarely two important factors. Far more important than anything around is the quality of food coupled with tense living that have made all the difference.

Another important observation which merits attention is that there is marked difference between the health standard of different caste families, and also between poor and rich families. It is seen that Scheduled Caste children and adults are the hungriest and suffer the most from severe malnutrition. Children of the small cultivators and those of landless labourers are also severely affected. It, however, does not mean that there is no malnutrition among the rich. That is also there but the causes and reasons are not the scarcity of good food and lack of money but wrong choices and bad food habits.

It is worth mentioning that most of the people in the village take three meals a day during summer, while two meals during the winter season. All the castes, by and large, are vegetarian. Some families of Scheduled Castes and also a few other take meat but only occasionally. The staple food of the entire village is wheat and bajra bread. It is taken day in and day out with monotonous regularity in combination with pulses vegetables, gur, shakar, lassi, chatni and onion. Pudding, porridge, *khichri*, *dalia* and *rabri* preparations also form a part of the food but taken either by the old or the sick. Special foods are prepared on the eve of festivals.

We shall now examine through Table 4.2 the diet pattern of the villagers in terms of conceivable food items.

Table 4.2 reveals that consumption of milk per average family is 4.4 litres which means 1.21 pints per capita. It is also evident that 25 per cent of the milk produced in the village is sold out in the city or the milk plant and little is left for the villagers. Earlier, it was a taboo for the farmers to sell milk. In fact, selling milk was considered inauspicious. But now several families sell milk. The per capita availability of milk is deplorable among certain castes such as Baniya, Punjabi, Sonar and Balmiki. Even in the case of landed families higher yield of milk means putting more money in the father's pocket and not necessarily more milk in the mouth of children,

Tea has almost replaced milk and *lassi* in the village. The tea habit is gaining ground very rapidly. Nearly 50 per cent of the families prepare and take tea two to three times daily round the year. Earlier, tea was preferred during the winter season and that too in the morning. Tea in excess quantity, is definitely a health hazard. Sadly enough, tea is served equally to the children without bothening for the evil effect it will have on their growth. It is worth mentioning that physical and mental growth of a child is qualitatively founded in the first six years of life. And if the child is not given enough quantity of milk and good food during these years then he will not catch up in later years. Unfortunately, even those who can afford milk

TABLE 4.2

Consumption of Some Selected Food Items Per Household (Kgs./litres)

Caste	Milk Consumed	Milk Sold	Ghee Desi	Ghee Vegetable	Mustard Oil	Gram	Sugar	Gur and Shakar	No. of Families Preparing Vegetables Daily
Ahir	4.0	4.0	2.0	—	1.0	—	6.0	5.0	—
Brahman	6.0	1.0	4.0	1.0	1.7	2.0	5.7	4.0	11
Jat	6.3	2.0	4.0	2.0	2.7	2.0	7.0	4.8	32
Saini	6.5	1.6	3.0	1.7	2.3	1.0	6.0	3.3	15
Baniya	1.0	—	2.0	1.5	1.0	—	6.0	—	1
Punjabi	1.0	—	1.0	3.0	1.0	—	4.0	—	1
Khati	3.5	3.0	1.0	1.5	0.4	—	4.8	2.0	1
Kumhar	2.0	3.0	0.8	—	0.2	—	7.0	2.0	1
Lohar	5.0	4.0	2.0	2.0	1.0	—	6.0	3.0	1
Nai	3.3	4.0	2.0	2.0	1.3	—	5.0	2.0	1
Sonar	1.0	—	2.0	1.5	1.5	—	9.0	2.0	1
Bairagi	4.0	2.0	1.5	1.8	1.0	—	3.7	3.2	4
Doom	5.5	0.7	2.0	2.5	2.1	—	4.6	1.4	9
Chamar	3.5	1.5	1.5	2.6	1.5	—	4.7	1.6	10
Balmiki	2.0	1.2	2.1	2.3	1.2	—	3.2	1.2	5
Total/	—	—	—	—	—	—	—	—	93
Weighted Average	4.4	1.8	2.4	1.3	1.4	1.8	5.6	3.3	—

Note : Consumption of food items excepting mustard oil is per month. In case of mustard oil, it is annual consumption,

are rapidly switching over to tea. It has become almost a fashion to serve tea even to the guests to whom only milk used to be served earlier. In many families even within the poorest ones one can see tea-sets and service trays which used to be a rarity in the village two decades ago.

Consumption of desi ghee per family works out 2.4 kg. per month. As in case of milk, consumption of ghee is more in case of Brahmins and Jats as compared to other castes. The consumption of vegetable ghee is relatively higher in the Punjabi and Scheduled Caste families. In case of Scheduled Castes, vegetable ghee supplements the requirements of desi ghee. The consumption of mustard oil per family is 1.4 kg. per annum, it being the highest for Jats followed by Sainis. Consumption of gram, gur and shakar has declined significantly. One does not hear of *missi-roti* any more. It has disappeared completely from the village menu excepting a few who have it occasionally. The consumption of gram in any other form has also become considerably low. Iron-rich jaggery, once produced and consumed amply has given way to calcium-free white sugar. Sugar intake in rich households far more exceeds that of poor families. Poor families find it difficult to afford even gur and shakar. It is alarming that gur and gram have almost disappeared from the diet of the villagers. Two decades ago, any villager could have these things. Even if gram and gur are available in the village, these are beyond the reach of poor households. It is surprising to know that out of a total of 371 families in the village, only 93 families consume any vegetables daily. The villagers do not care to grow vegetables whereas they can easily reserve a part of their holdings for seasonal vegetable crops such as lady-finger, gourd, carrots, radish etc. Many of the landed families look upon the cultivation of vegetable crops as a degrading occupation. In all, the diet of the people remains far from balanced, for want of vegetables and fruit.

It is quite distressing to note growing liquor addiction which is eating into the very vitals of rural health. There has been a manifold increase in the consumption of liquor in the village during the last decade. Many a village elder decry this trend but to the younger generation it is a fashionable way to bridge the gap between the urban and rural way of life. Though, there is no wine shop in the village as such but it is easily available either from a *theka* in the nearby village named Kiloi or from Rohtak. Now, however, it is learnt that wine shop has been removed from Kiloi on the request of village Panchayat.

It is evident from the foregoing analysis that owing to poverty and due to wrong choices of food items the physical standard in the village is deteriorating rapidly. We need not give several pages of statistics to be convinced of this. One can go to this village and see the conditions for one self how children, adults and old people suffer from malnutrition and consequent infirmities and ailments.

Festivals

Festivals play a significant role in the village life. These refresh the lives of the villagers and provide an opportunity to the village community to come closer with each other. Among the important festivals celebrated in the village include Holi, Dussehra, Diwali, Rakhi, Teej, Krishnasthami, Makar Sankranti, and Shivaratri. A brief description of various festivals is presented as under :

Holi : Holi is one of the very important festivals, celebrated in the village. This festival falls on Purnima (full moon light) in the month of Falgun (March-April). Holi is celebrated by the entire village with much fun and gusto. It is a festival of merry-making and revelry. The children and youth of the village collect and pile dry wood and cow-dung cakes at two or three points outside the village, much in advance of Holi, and Holi fire is lit toward the evening on this day. The next day, Holi is celebrated and the whole village rejoices by participating in funny games without any distinction of caste and creed. Water, plain or colour-mixed, is sprinkled by the ladies over their menfolk. The practice of splashing water which used to be a full month affair in Falgun in yester-years is now restricted only to a few days preceding Holi. Children in groups throw coloured water on one another. Besides these festivities ladies sing traditional songs in sympathy of Holi.

Indeed, Holi is a festival of joy and merriment, of unity and cordiality of inter-caste and inter-family relations, and is celebrated by young and old alike. Women, besides slinging mud water also give a beating to their menfolk with rope hunter and wooden stick. Women chasing their menfolk and doing beating and the men running in defence in front of them is quite hilarious to watch and a common scene during these days. On this occasion, people feast on sumptuous dishes and decorate their houses. Unfortunately, some celebrate the festival by taking heavy doses of wine and then pick a quarrel leading to untoward incident in the village.

Dussehra : The festival of Dussehra falls 20 days ahead of Diwali in the month of October. This festival is also known as festival of sacrifice, and people celebrate the victory of the mythical Rama over the demon king of Lanka-Ravana. Celebration of Dussehra, in fact, commences ten days preceding this day and the entire period of celebration is marked by gaiety and rejoicing. The whole village hums with a new life and assumes a festive look with men, women and children clad in their new and best clothes. A large number of villagers go to Rohtak city to enjoy Ramlila which is staged in different localities of the city. The Ramlila comes to an end on the tenth day corresponding to Dussehra when the effigies of Ravna, Megnad, Kumbhakaran and other demons is set on fire in the evening. Another festival named 'Sanjhi' is also celebrated on the same evening when young girls of the village float 'Sanjhi' secretly in the ponds or rivers of the village in earthen pots.

Diwali : Like Dussehra it is one of the important festivals celebrated with zest and gaiety in the village. The festival falls on Amavasya in the month of Kartik (October-November). Fire-works are displayed. Each family cleans and white washes its house. The interior is decorated with pictures and other agents bought from the city. Mud houses and the Kucha floor of Pucca houses are smeared with cow-dung. Cattle are thoroughly bathed, their horns are decorated in fitting colours. The e are also decked with gandli—a two feet long rope interwoven with coloured cotton threads and cuttings mopped with peacock feathers collected from the fields for this occasion. It is a day of special menu ; Khir, Halwa, Puri and good vegetables are delicacies. People enjoy the evening with hard drinks. People of this village are of the belief that this festival is celebrated to perpetuate the memory of Lord Rama who returned to Ayodhya after the long exile of 14 years. A day before Diwali, another festival named *Girdi* is also celebrated when children receive sweets and other special eatables from their parents. The festival of Girdi is also known as *Chotti Diwali.* No sufficient reason for its celebration is given by the villagers except that preparations to celebrate Diwali commence from this day and hence this is appropriately called '*Chotti Diwali*'.

Gowardhan Puja takes place the following day. In this manner, the festival of Diwali has three consecutive festivals namely, the Girdi, Diwali and Gowardhan Puja. There is a popular myth that Lord Krishna lifted on his palm the Gowardhan mountain. Its location is said to be near Mathura and the Lord lifted it to protect the grazing cattle of the village from the wrath of Lord Indra—God of rains. So a Gowardhan, i.e., a symbolic mountain carved out of cow-dung is worshipped by offering milk, curd and rice. Gowardhan Puja is mainly performed by womenfolk, and men generally do not participate. Children are also not interested in this excepting that there is a model of Gowardhan of cow-dung in their houses which adds to their curiosity and amazement.

Teej : Teej is an important seasonal festival of the village which is celebrated on the third day of the bright fortnight of Sawan. It is the festival of swings and sweet fried foods. On this occasion, women and children appear in their best, wear ornaments and enjoy swinging in nearby trees. Adults also do not lag behind. They also participate in swinging competition towards the evening and there is a lot of fun and frolic. Children, much in advance, reserve the suitable branches of the trees where their swings could be hung on the eve of this day. Ladies swing in groups and sing traditional songs on the occasion. Newly married girls get gifts of new clothes, sweets and other articles from their father-in-law. This package of gift is popularly known as *Sindhara* in local dialect. Ladies prepare a variety of foods with great enthusiasm. The main cooking medium is mustard oil and the delicacies include Puri, Gulgale, Suhali, Shakarpare, etc.

Rakhi : Rakhi or Raksha-Bandhan falls on the last day of the month of Sawan. People do not know exactly how this festival came into being though there are different versions of it. Rakhi is a multicoloured thread and is tied to the wrist of a brother by his sister. The thread is considered to be a symbol of safety against any evil in future. The sisters are then given presents and gifts by the brothers in cash and kind on this day. On occasions the gift is not less than some milch cattle—a buffalo or a cow. Rakhi is also sent by post to the brothers who serve at distance places and could not be present on the occasion.

Krishnasthami : Krishnashthami falls on the eighth day of Bhadva (August-September). As in the rest of Haryana and several other states in the country, this festival is celebrated with faith and interest. It is believed that it was the day when Lord Krishna incarnated himself. People, mostly females, observe the day long fast until the moon is sighted at mid night. After seeing the moon, people break their fast with some light sweets and other food items. Children are also seen observing this lengthy and difficult fast, but that is more for sweet and *geewar* (a kind of sweet) and less for religious purposes.

Sankranti : This festival falls during the winter season on 13th January every year and is observed by all the communities in the village. It is significant to note that all and sundry in the village take an early morning bath almost ritualistically. In fact, bath is a must before breakfast. It is common belief among the villagers that one who fails to take bath on this day will incarnate as donkey in the next birth. It is a day of delicious foods. There is a tradition that dogs are particularly fed liberally. Ladies, particularly the newly married ones, coa their elders to accept clothes blanket and even money from them as a token of respect. While performing this ceremony ladies approach their elders, who pretend to hide in other's houses, singing in group and offer the gift. All are in a jubilant and gayful mood.

Shivratri : It falls on the fourth day of the dark fortnight of Falgun. On the eve of this festival men, women and children worship Lord Shiva to seek His blessings. People worship the Lord in Shivalayas with all obeisance and pomp. Fast is also observed on this day and women outnumber menfolk in this respect. As noted earlier in Chapter 2, since there is no big Shivalya in the village, the villagers go to nearby Shivalaya at Kiloi village for the purpose. At Kiloi, a big fair is held on the eve of Shivratri, and devotees from various villages flock together to take part in it. Women overwhelmingly attend it and sing devotional songs in praise of Shivjee. It is worth remarking here that Shivjee is their supreme deity and the villagers rever and worship this with full devotion.

Kartika Purnima : It falls on the last day of Kartika month. This Purnima is awaited eagerly by the children and ladies in the village as they have the words and assurances from the elderly persons in the familly who will take them for bathing to the Ganga or the Jamuna river, which are considered very sacred by the Hindus. And hundreds of villagers go to distant places like Garhgange and Hardwar to have a dip an the Gangees or alternatively to Jamuna (Delhi and other places) for a holy bath. Most of them travel to these places in groups by tractors, with all the necessary provisions of a week or so. On their return, they fetch with them sacred water of these rivers and also the *Parsad* which is distributed among the villagers. Children buy toys and other play-goods from the fairs which are held on the occasion.

Kanagats : Kanagats are observed for fifteen days in the first fortnight of Ausoj by worshipping their dead ancestors and offering them water, bread, rice etc. For fifteen days people lead an austere life. On the day of *Sharadh* they offer oblations to the departed souls and feed the Brahmins sumptuously. But now Brahmins do not get as much importance as they used to in old days during the Kanagats.

Marriages

Marriages are performed strictly within one's own caste and there is not a single case of inter-caste marriage reported from the village. The marriages, by and large, are an arranged affair i.e. selection of mates is finalised by the parents rather than by the marriage partners themselves. Of late, family members alongwith the boy insist to see the girl and other things before the finalisation of betrothal ceremony. That is, in many castes, the approval of the boy is necessary before the marriage negotiations are completed. Earlier, Brahmin or Nai used to make all these enquiries, and the boy and members of the family were not required to see the girl before marriage. This practice had resulted in incompatitible marriages in many cases in the village.

It is to be emphasised that still the girl has hardly any say in the matter of choosing the bridegroom. She is expected to be obedient to the parents in selecting the bridegroom in all the castes in the village. A sort of precondition is taken that the girl is younger than the boy at least by 2 to 4 years. Virginity and character of the girl is the single most important factor and the bridegroom's family almost always seeks to verify the gri's antecedents before betrothal is accepted. As already mentioned, marriage does not take place within the same sub-caste or lineage. Not only this, in most of the castes in the village three sub-castes—that of the boy, the boy's mother, as also that of his grand-mother are srictly avoided. There is no case of marriage in which the wife belongs to the same village or the adjacent or neighbouring villages.

Another noticeable feature of marriage in the village now is that child marriage has become quite rare. The appropriate age for marriage for the boy and the girl is considered by the villagers to be at least 18 and 21 respectively. There are also many cases of late marriage in the village. The practice of late marriage is very comon among the educated young men who wait for marriage until they are well settled in life. Even in case of Scheduled Castes which are supposed to favour an early marriage, the age of marriage favoured by them has gone up considerably.

It is to be admitted that marriages have become quite expensive. No doubt, factors like land, reputation of the family, education and job are preferential qualifications for marriage but dowry is yet another important consideration. A family, other conditions being equal, that can give maximum dowry to the bridegroom's family is preferred to others. But fortunately, however, this practice hardly finds currency with the highly educated young men. This condition is also relaxed if the girl is beautiful and educated. Views condemning dowry system are expressed by all but it is not put to practice by many. Dowry items, among the poor and medium include bicycle, watch, sewing machine and radio-set, while in case of a well-off family scooter, motor-cycle, dress suits and other clothes, television-set, double-bed, steel almirah and fridge are the popular items for dowry.

Marriages in the village are generally performed during the months of May and June after the harvesting and threshing of wheat crop is over. Though marriages are also solemnized during other months but May and June are the usual months for marriages. For transporting marriage parties, cars and buses are hired. The use of taxis and buses to transport marriage parties has become a status symbol. Heavily over-loaded cars with their cargo of garlands, grooms and others are a common sight in the months of May and June in the village. Those who are less privileged or parsimonions by nature use tractors, scooters and four-wheelers for the purpose. The use of carts for transporting marriage parties is out of fashion and now stands virtually discarded.

Caste Relations

There are, as we are aware, 15 castes in the village. The relations between castes in the village, on the whole, are cordial. There has not been on record any violent and serious confrontation between castes. The main feuds that occurred in the village in the past years were intra-caste rather than inter-caste. Although, there are now fewer caste restrictions yet the system of caste discrimination still continues. We can see in the village, young men and women performing several tasks together unmindful of their castes. To be together in the village schools is one of the biggest helps in this direction. There are only two inhibitions which separate the castes. First, several castes do not feel free to accept food from the lower and Scheduled Castes. Secondly, people do not consider marry-ing anyone outside their own caste. These two conventions, as they stand today, however, do not interfere with inter-personal relationships between people of different castes.

We find the village farmers of higher castes working shoulder to shoulder with their Scheduled Caste labourers.

They don't feel awkward about these close contact meetings in the process of work. An uninformed observer watching these men working together might find it difficult to know that they were separated by a caste. In most cases the farmer provides meals to the low caste labourers which are brought to the fields by some one from the farmer and the low caste labourers eat their food squating on the ground and all distances are forgotten. The children of all castes play together like children everywhere without remembering any caste distinction. In schools also, they sit and learn together.

The socio-economic status of the untouchables has also undergone some change during the 40 years of independence due to government policy. The government has been doing everything legally possible to remove their stigma. In official statements they are now referred to as the Scheduled Castes and not *Harijans*. Measures have been introduced to raise their social and economic status. They are encouraged to make use of government assistance which facilitates their education from primary school through college and university. These facilities have been availed of mostly by the Chamars in the village whereas Balmikis have remained vastly unaffected by the measures.

During the course of survey of the village, we also tried to assess the attitude of the villagers towards the Scheduled Castes. The results, which are presented in Table 4.3, are quite interesting and instructive.

Table 4.3 indicates that about 60 per cent of the households believe in caste identity, the proportion who believe in the system, as expected, being quite high among the high castes like Brahmins and Jats. However, those educated and in service amongst these castes are mostly freer from such an attitude. Regarding the concessions given by the government to these castes one-third consider these concessions necessary for the upliftment of the lower castes, the rest being against any ameliorative measures. There is silent opposition from certain castes to the granting of concessions to Backward and Scheduled Castes. When asked about the inter-caste marriage, it was favoured hardly by one-fifth families mostly of the low castes. High

TABLE 4.3
Attitude Towards Scheduled Castes

Caste	Believing in Caste System	Favouring Concessions to S.C.	Favouring Inter-Caste Marriages	Willing to Invite S.C. to Special Functions
Ahir	1	—	—	—
Brahmin	24	—	—	—
Jat	130	9	21	32
Saini	22	—	—	—
Baniya	—	—	—	—
Punjabi	—	—	—	—
Khati	—	—	—	—
Kumhar	—	—	—	—
Lohar	—	1	1	1
Nai	—	3	3	3
Sonar	3	1	—	—
Bairagi	6	5	—	—
Doom	4	13	6	6
Chamar	15	50	41	30
Balmiki	16	45	40	20
Total	221	127	112	92
Percentage	59.6	34.2	30.2	24.8

Note : S.C. indicates Scheduled Caste.

castes families, by and large, with the exception of 21 Jat families presently opposed the idea of inter-caste marriages. Similarly, there is not much of interaction among castes on the occasions of celebrating social functions.

Habits

Table 4.4 demonstrates the habits of the households in the village.

It is evident from Table 4.4 that the habits of smoking and tea drinking are quite strong among the households in the village. About 76 per cent of the households reported the habit of smoking among its members. A little more than one-third of the house prepare tea daily even during the summer season. Regard-houseing the social taboo of veiling, nearly 80 per cent families observe this system whereas only 20 per cent did not see any point in the observance of this. They look on it as useless and practice. However, the system of veiling is not followed very strictly by educated women-folk who are in service particularly in the cities. It was also noticed that litigation and some other harmful activities had been going on in the village. There are, at present, 28 cases of avoidable litigation in the village. This reflects on the poor functioning of the Panchayat in the settlement of disputes in the village. The major source of entertainment in the village is radio listening and card playing. Surprisingly, sports don't find favour with the village youth. The sports facilities in the village are not worth the name. Reading of newspaper and other creative and standard literature is also very uncommon among the villagers. Those who read, read only cheap novels and are not aware of the standard literary works.

Panchayat

The Panchayat is expected to play a significant role in the overall development of the village. For any positive success, village development should start with the full participation of the villagers. Their active participation is expected to generate a new experience and self-confidence. This, however, does not rule out assistance from outside. All put together, the capacity of the village community to grow from within should be the first and foremost consideration. By and lage the Panchayat

TABLE 4.4
Some Habits of the Households

Caste	Households Reporting Smoking	Households Who Prepare Tea Daily	Veiling System	Liti-gation	Radio Listening	Card Playing
Ahir	1	—	2	—	—	—
Brahmin	26	5	27	1	10	6
Jat	137	100	122	26	101	20
Saini	24	6	28	1	12	4
Baniya	—	—	1	—	—	—
Punjabi	—	—	—	—	1	—
Khati	1	—	1	—	1	1
Kumhar	2	—	3	—	1	1
Lohar	1	—	2	—	1	—
Nai	3	—	3	—	2	—
Sonar	3	1	3	—	1	1
Bairagi	6	1	6	—	1	2
Doom	4	2	13	—	4	2
Chamar	30	5	40	—	10	5
Balmiki	45	6	45	—	8	6
Total	233	126	296	28	153	48
Percentage	76.3	34.0	79.8	7.5	41.2	13.0

aims at fulfilling these objectives. The political power and authority in the village are vested in the village Panchayat. Panchayat membership is open to all, without being the prerogative of the influential few, belonging to privileged castes and families. The Panchayat is no more an office of hereditary leaders. The elections are held through secret ballot. The weaker sections of society, including Scheduled Castes and women, are given special representation in the Panchayat. As indicated earlier in Chapter 2, the number of Scheduled Caste and lady members in Ladhot Panchayat is three and one respectively. Some other relevant details pertaining to the members are reproduced in Table 4.5.

It is obvious from Table 4.5 that nearly all the major castes in the village are represented on the Panchayat and membership cuts across caste boundaries. As already discussed in Chapter 2, the Panchayat in Ladhot has undertaken some developmental work and has been functioning satisfactorily. The Panchayat is entrusted with significant powers. It deals with small matters both insignificant and important, ranging from such matters as squabbles over a small pit in the street to questions of shares in property, boundaries of fields etc. It has also to perform several obligatory duties like construction, repair and maintenance of village streets, public wells, tanks, sanitation etc. Besides, there are certain discretionary duties including cooperation, promotion and development of economic conditions with special reference to agriculture, establishment and maintenance of dispensaries, maternity and child welfare centres etc.

The procedure for convening the Panchayat meeting in the village is simple. The aggrieved person calls the elected Panchayat and other village folk who generally assemble in the village chaupal preferably in the evening. The other party and those who have witnessed the occurrence are sent for and are heard patiently. After listening to all the parties, the members then give their decision unanimously or by majority which is very often obeyed by all. If the parties fail to carry the judgement of the panchayat then they are advised to go to the court of law. The witnesses are administered an oath of *Gangajee* in the Panchayat before they give the evidence. It has been observed that in many cases moral pressure of the

TABLE 4.5

Composition of Village Panchayat

Sr. No.	Name	Designation	Caste	Age	Sex	Education	Land (Hectares)
1.	Deewan Singh	Sarpanch	Jat	50	Male	Middle	1.0
2.	Kaul Dass	Member	-do-	51	-do-	Illiterate	6.0
3.	Sawrupi	-do-	-do-	70	Female	-do-	1.4
4.	Ram Dutt	-do-	Brahmin	42	Male	-do-	1.0
5.	Rajender	-do-	Sunar	28	-do-	Primary	Nil
6.	Ram Kishan	-do-	Chamar	34	-do-	Middle	Nil
7.	Banara	-do-	Balmiki	45	-do-	Illiterate	Nil
8.	Hoshiar	-do-	-do-	35	-do-	-do-	Nil

Panchayat on the concerned proves quite effective in resolving the disputes.

It may be mentioned here that caste Panchayat now no longer plays any significant role in the social organisation of a villagc though they meet occasionally to consider major issues confronting a particular caste. For instance, more recently, in September, 1987, Deswals a sub-caste from several villages assembled at Gangoli village to sort out some matrimonial issue which had been agitating the minds of the people. The decision adopted by the caste Panchayat to fine the defaulting party was carried out faithfully. But such assemblage is quite rare and takes place only when the caste is threatened with some quarrel leading to far-reaching consequences or common problem. Similar caste Panchayat of Deswals was reported to be held in Anta and Kurar villages in the past. As the caste Panchayat can perform several functions and take action against individuals or groups ranging from imposition of fine to ex-communication, this proves a deterrent to the people in committing serious social mistakes and crimes.

Reverting back to the functioning of statutory Panchayat, it is unfortunate that the Panchayat endowed with legal and fiscal powers, expected to take the lead in self-help has been the victim of circumstances in the village. Admittedly, some developmental works have been performed by the Ladhot Panchayat as referred to in Chapter 2 but much more could have been done. What then has been the bane of Panchayat in the village ? The financial limitations and factionalism in the village are the two important factors which tend to hinder the smooth functioning of the Panchayat and limit its role in the socio-economic transformation of the village.

The finances of the Panchayat are meager and hence the works on wider scale cannot be executed. The total income of Ladhot Panchayat for the 1985-1986 was only Rs. 22232 and the expenditure incurred was to the tune of Rs. 23819 leaving a deficit of Rs. 1587 during the year under reference. A breakdown of income and expenditure is set out in Table 4.6.

Evidently much developmental work in the village could not be undertaken due to the paucity of funds. There is urgent need to find financial resources for Panchayat in order to enlarge the scope of its developmental activities.

TABLE 4.6

Income and Expenditure of Ladhot Panchayat 1985-86

INCOME			EXPENDITURE		
Sr. No.	Particulars	Amount Rs.	Sr. No.	Particulars	Amount Rs.
1.	Govt. Grants	10,000	1.	School and Streets	20,320.00
2.	House-tax	6,589	2.	Agriculture	3,224.00
3.	Revenue from Samlat Land	3,600	3.	Contingency	275.00
4.	Miscellaneous	2,043			
	Total	22,232			23,819.00

Source : B.D.O. Office, Rohtak.

Another important factor which obviates the working of the Panchayat is the factionalism in the village. There are several faction leaders in the village. Sometimes, these village leaders vehemently oppose the Panchayat resulting in a complete chaos in the Panchayat administration and slowing down the village developmental programmes. Infact, the success of development works depends on the joint approval of both the caste and village leaders and the Panchayat. If the common agreement is not reached at, the progress of the village remains stand-still. The present Panchayat is handicapped in undertaking some development activities for want of support from the actual leaders of the village who are split in two rival groups ever since the Panchayat elections. The Panchayat requires the maximum cooperation of the leaders. Leaders are expected to consider the order and well-being of the community rather than their personal ambitions. No doubt, the burden of responsibility rests on the leader just as family responsibility rests on the head of the household. The moment, a villager finds himself harassed by other fellow villager or by the police implicating him in concocted cases, naturally he comes either to his leader or Panchayat expecting the necessary help. financial or otherwise. It becomes the duty of the leader to represent his case to the Panchayat on merit and should not be overwhelmed by caste and other considerations. But the village leaders who are wealthy and influential seem to be linked with wider political system and they are politically articulated to embarrass the Panchayat.

A careful examination would reveal that the Panchayat in Ladhot has a limited success in attaining its objectives. Actually, the Panchayat should become an agency for quick social and economic reform rather than an institution dominated by various types of vested interests. *Lok Adalat*, a new type of institution which is being heard recently, has no impact on village life. Lok Adalat is a village court which can decide both civil and criminal cases and also fine defaulters. It appears from the press that Lok Adalat which has met in Rohtak district at various places has been able to resolve many disputes. But as far as this village is concerned, no case has ever been taken by its residents to the Lok Adalat.

CHAPTER 5

DEVELOPMENT PROGRAMMES, PEOPLES' RESPONSE, CONSCIOUSNESS AND AWARENESS

In India the bulk of population is rural and, therefore, no popular government can afford to neglect rural development programmes. However, the execution of such programmes is not an easy task. It is bristled with problems and difficulties. In villages there tends to be heavy pressure of population on scarce land, facilities like irrigation and transportation are not adequate, health and educational facilities are lacking, non-farm occupations are not well-developed, and institutions like banking and marketing are very small in number. Not only this, the situation further gets accentuated and becomes worse due to the luke warm and conventional attitudes of the majority of rural population towards the rural upliftment programmes. To initiate rural development programmes and to ensure their success, happen to be crucial stages for the betterment of rural population. Certainly, merely the initiation of rural development programmes would not be sufficient, it is absolutely necessary that rural population respond to these programmes favourably and are conscious and aware of the problems faced by them.

This chapter investigates the issues outlined above in respect of Ladhot village. It is made clear at the very outset that since it is beyond the scope of this project to analyse all the social development programmes which have been launched since independence, we would concentrate only on a few important ones in the solution of social problems. Since agriculture forms the backbone of the village economy we discuss mainly the programmes which have bearing on the village agriculture. These include land ceiling programmes, high yielding varieties programme, community development and other similar programmes.

Land Ceiling

Land ceiling has been one of the most controversial aspects in the whole gamut of Land Reform measures in India. It envisaged that beyond a certain specified limit, all lands belonging to big land-lords will be taken over by the State and allotted to landless households to enable them to meet their growing demands through land. However, owing to certain loop-holes and exemptions in the ceiling law, no land could be declared surplus in the village. As already seen in Chapter 2 the size of the land-holdings in the village is not big enough and these remained outside the ambit of ceiling. The only two-three big farmers who had land beyond the ceiling limit at that time managed mala fide transfers of their lands and easily evaded the ceiling laws. Obviously, there remained loop-holes within the legal provisions and ceiling laws could easily be by passed. Thus, the very objective of land reforms and the provision of ceiling were watered down in the process of implementation. Now, there is no surplus land in the entire village and land ceiling measure turned out be redundent completely. The land reform has been successful in the village only to the extent that scattered holdings could be consolidated in compact plots at two or three points around the village. This has encouraged the farmers to take agriculture seriously and enabled them to undertake long term investment activities on their farms. This, in fact, has made the farmers more receptive to new technology and methods of cultivation besides saving their time and energies.

We also elicited the views of the villagers regarding land ceiling which are presented in the Table 5.1.

Table 5.1 portrays clearly that more than 30 per cent of the villagers had not even heard about the land ceiling measures. Out of those who had heared about it, more than 50 per eent

TABLE 5.1

Views Regarding Ceiling

Caste	Who have heard about land ceiling		Who favour land ceiling		To whom should the surplus land go			
					to small farmers		to landless	
Ahir	2	(67)	0	(0)	0	(0)	0	(0)
Brahmin	25	(81)	20	(65)	20	(100)	0	(0)
Jat	116	(76)	82	(54)	70	(85)	12	(15)
Saini	25	(76)	20	(61)	20	(100)	0	(0)
Baniya	1	(100)	1	(100)	1	(100)	0	(0)
Punjabi	1	(100)	1	(100)	1	(100)	0	(0)
Khati	5	(53)	5	(63)	3	(60)	2	(40)
Kumhar	5	(71)	4	(57)	2	(50)	2	(50)
Lohar	10	(77)	7	(54)	4	(57)	3	(43)
Nai	2	(67)	1	(33)	1	(100)	0	(0)
Sonar	2	(67)	1	(33)	1	(100)	0	(0)
Bairagi	4	(57)	4	(57)	2	(50)	2	(50)
Doom	7	(54)	7	(54)	5	(71)	2	(29)
Chamar	30	(67)	25	(56)	0	(0)	25	(100)
Balmiki	20	(40)	20	(40)	0	(0)	20	(100)
Total	255	(69)	198	(53)	130	(66)	68	(34)

Note : Figures in parenthesis indicate percentages.

of the individual approved of the land ceiling measure and the rest disapproved of it. Among the castes, Jats and Sainis overwhelmingly did not favour it. A larger proportion of households opined that the surplus land, if any, should go to the marginal and small farmers, so as to make those units of farming more viable. They argued that if the land is transferred to the landless households then it would automatically result in dissipation of the resources employed in agriculture and would lead to serious social tensions in the village. On the contrary, however, non-cultivating castes, by and large, wanted to share village land and favoured equal re-distribution of the entire village land.

High Yielding Variety Programme and Green Revolution

Since the inception of Haryana as a separate state in Novermber 1966, the traditional agricultural practices are gradually being replaced by modern technology and new farm practices. Initially, the new technology was tried as a pilot project in Intensive Agricultural District Programme (IADP) Karnal. Later, more districts including Rohtak were covered under it. The High Yielding Varieties Programme (HYVP) was also added to the IADP which resulted in what is now termed as 'Green Revolution'. Green revolution embodied in the seed-fertiliser-irrigation package. Regarding the emergence of green revolution, it would be too optimistic and premature to assert that it has already taken place in the village in its full form. The agricultural improvement and the partial success of green revolution in the village appears largely due to the adoption of better quality seeds and the use of chemical fertilizers.

Let us now first analyse the success of the HYVP in this village. A discussion on fertilizers would also be a attempted further in this chapter. The Haryana Agricultural University, Hissar has been trying hard to evolve and popularise improved and disease-resisting varieties of seeds suitable for different local conditions in the state. There have also been private producers who multiply foundation seeds and certify quality seeds under the prescribed quality control arrangements. Consequently, a number of high yielding varieties of wheat, rice, bajra, sugarcane and certain vegetables and fodders have been evolved. Because of this development, the area coverage under high yielding varieties in the village rose from almost nil in 1968-69 to 50 per cent in 1985-86. However, except for wheat (varieties 1953 and 47) and to some extent bajra (Kothliwala or sankar bajra) and paddy (IR 8), the coverage under HYV seeds is still very low.

It would be pertinent at this stage to assess the success and the difficulties of the farmers in the adoption of HYVP in the village. HYVP as reported earlier, was quickly adopted by most of the farmers irrespective of the size of their holding. This amply proves that most of the farmers in the village are receptive to new agricultural technology. All the same there one many problems which bother the farmers in carrying out this programme. Table 5.2 brings this fact out.

Table 5.2 brings out the nature and magnitude of the problem in respect of the adoption of HYVP in terms of three size groups of holdings. Procuring good quality seed, surprisingly, appears to be the most acute problem more so with small and bigger farms. There is no seed store in the village. And the seed varieties which the farmers are able to get from different places and sources are not fully tested with a full sense of responsibility. There is virtually no accountability and no one has any stake in success or failure of new variety delivered to the farmers. Next to the problem of procurement of seed is the problem of marketing particularly in HYV wheat. But in recent years with the launching of the liberal government policy, the problem of marketing has became easy. Marketing of HYV wheat was really a problem during the late sixties and early seventies when it was just introduced. Even now the market prices of the new varieties of wheat are lower than those of the traditional ones. Susceptibility presented the next acute problem, more so in case of small farmers who cannot afford to use pesticides in the eventuality of crop disease. For fear of the disease farmers would like to grow old varieties (excepting wheat) as these are generally disease free and ensure sure return to the subsistence farmers. Next, farmers again the small ones were handicapped in the matter of fertilizers, lack of finance, power supply and labour

TABLE 5.2

Farmers Who Faced Difficulties in Cultivation of High Yielding Varieties of Crops

Difficulty Faced in Respect of	Small	Medium	Large	Total
Procurement of seed	133 (95)	36 (71)	21 (95)	190 (89)
Fertilizers	105 (75)	30 (59)	19 (86)	154 (72)
Water shortage	126 (90)	26 (51)	13 (59)	165 (77)
Power shortage	85 (61)	37 (73)	13 (59)	135 (63)
Labour shortage	27 (19)	21 (41)	7 (32)	55 (26)
Lack of finance	102 (73)	31 (61)	14 (64)	147 (69)
Marketing	127 (91)	39 (76)	18 (82)	184 (86)
Suceptibility	127 (91)	38 (75)	16 (73)	181 (85)

Note : Figures in parentheses are percentages of total land owing farmers in each category such as small 140, medium 51, large 22 and tatal 213.

shortage in that order constituted handicaps in adoption of HYV programme. Labour shortage, understandably, was more of a problem with large farms notwithstanding the level of mechanisation which saves labour. The same is true in caste of finance.

It is gratifying to note that farmers seem to have found the new varieties profitable enough, as 100 per cent farmers were ready to continue to grow the new varieties provided some problems are removed and tackled properly by the government and other agencies. It might be mentioned that only a few farmers, whose number is negligible, suffered from sheer prejudice against HYV seeds, indicating that the programme has bright future and farmers are amenable to change. Keeping in view the difficulties enumerated above, government should ensure adequate and timely supply of seeds and fertilizers, make provision of credit for purchase of supporting inputs on easy terms and purchase the entire produce at fairly reasonably remunerative price.

Community Development and Other Programmes

The idea of community development was mooted as a part of the decentralised approach to rural development. Community Development approach often led to the establishment of rural local government institutions as agencies of rural development. Ladhot is included in Rohtak block which has its headquarters at Rohtak itself. Clearly, the Block Development Officer (BDO) is an important official for the villages under his charge but it is unusual for him to find time to visit all the villages at sufficient intervals and Ladhot is no exception.

The Commuity Development efforts in the village were not of sufficient nature since many activities required for rural development remained only on papers. The villagers further complained that whatever benefits were there, these were cornered by the richer section of the rural community and a large majority of the rural population could not get even the fringe of these benefits. Because of this, people in the village have also developed indifferent and apathetic attitude towards Block activities. Therefore, it was but natural that hardly

10 per cent respondents ever visited their Block office at Rohtak.

Keeping in view the multifarious activities under the Community Development Programme, the government thought it expedient to introduce specific schemes which would direct more resources for a particular problem and a particular section of the rural community. This has resulted in many rural development programmes like Rural Works Programmes, Marginal Farmers and Agriculture Labourers Scheme, Small Farmers Development Agencies, Integrated Dry Land Agriculture Development, Agro-Service Centres, Area Development Schemes, Programme for Rural Employment, Food for work Programme, National Rural Employment Programme, Integrated Rural Development Programme, Training of Rural Youth for Self-Employment, and several others. But sadly enough even the well-meant programmes mentioned above have not resulted in any improvement the lot of the villagers. Many households in the village were found not even aware of the various development programmes run by the government. It is to be admitted that not enough efforts have gone into making these programmes effective and viable. These are not properly and adequately manned. No substantial and serious efforts, giving real attention to the problems of the villagers particularly the landless, small farmers and poorly educated persons, have begun in the village. No doubt, the scarce financial resources to implement these programmes have drained down.

It would be interesting to present the conflicting views and reactions of different strata of people in the village in regard to these rural programmes. It was discovered that more than half of the households remained unaffected by the various development programmes run by the government in the village. Many respondents were critical to the running of several programmes meant only for the Backward and Scheduled Castes. Many villagers further contested that these discriminatory programmes failed to bring about any improvement in their lot. Some others argued that benefits arising out of these programmes had gone only to the influential and rich persons and not to the common villager. Even the many

Scheduled Castes were not found quite satisfied with several programmes launched for them. Only a few admitted the usefulness of these programmes.

It may safely be concluded that the rural programmes have not proved very successful in meeting the objectives of rural development. It is alleged that the targets have been achieved only on papers and real beneficiaries were not the target groups and the poor. It was also reported by several beneficiaries of the programmes that subsidies for the creation of their productive assets involved a system of brokerage and corruption. In many cases, the asset creation approach in the programme failed in its objectives of income generating. The symbolic relationships between bureauracy of the development administration, credit institutions, and the leaders of the village are in their own ways, responsible for the failure of these programmes.

Naturally, the question is : what should be done to improve the situation so that the percolation effect of these programmes becomes more significant in the village ? The only answer lies in starting the field agencies and the rural institut-tions by competent people-educated, well trained with requisite qualification, skills and background. Special incentives are also necessary to attract competent personnel to the field of rural development. Such personnel need to be properly trained not only to impart requisite knowledge and skill but to develop proper attitudes. Thus, proper man power planning should form an integral part of the plan for rural development and its progress. The task of rural development cannot be accomplished by the field agencies of administrative departments alone. This should be linked with a vast network of rural institutions, co-operatives, rural institutions, co-operatives, rural banks, farmers' association, youth and women associations, etc.

Use of Resources and Technology

Labour and Power : It is observed that there is some degree of sub-optional use of available farm resources employed in village agriculture. As analysed in Chapter 3, the family labour on many farms is not fully utilized all the year round. Similarly, a large number of households did not make full use of their existing draft and tractor power. The practice of hiring out of family labour among the farming households is minimal. Only four households of Jats, who lent some of their family labour to fellow cultivators, due to miserable economic conditions, could be identified. Hiring out of surplus bullock labour is also not very much in vogue. Hardly four households in the entire village followed this practice. But in case of tractors, the hiring out was quite considerable. The tractor services were hired out to fellow cultivators in the village for different agricultural operations such as ploughing, drawing water from the tubewells, threshing, transporting the produce to markets, etc.

It may be mentioned that threshing of wheat is one of the major agricultural operations in the village. The threshing of wheat is largely done with threshing machine and the traditional methods of wheat threshing with the help of Phulsi are nowhere to be seen. Some rich and prudent farmers also, get their wheat crop harvested by the State-owned combined harvester which can reap, thresh and bag the grain, all in one operation, at a cost of Rs. 500 per hectare. But only one or two farmers utilized the services of combined harvester in the survey year.

Fertilizers : The consumption of chemical fertilizers in the village has increased over the time period. The basic aim in the application of chemical fertilizers is to maximise output per unit of land. The high level of consumption of fertilizer is also necessitated due to the adoption of HYVP. Truely, HYV responds very well to the application of fertilizers. It may be stated that chemical fertilizer was not quite new to the farmers in the village, albeit, they did not use it widely two decades ago. The position regarding present usage of fertilizer is presented through Table 5.3.

The Table 5.3 reveals that there is, as expected, remarkable level of difference in the use of fertilizers among different categories of farmers. The use of fertilizers per average cultivating farmer in the whole village works out to 7.6 bags. But there are wide variations around this average. The use of

TABLE 5.3

Fertilizer Consumption in Ladhot 1984-85

Category	Number of Farmers	Average Number of Bags
Small	140	4.4
Medium	51	8.0
Large	22	27.0
Total Weighted Average	213	7.6

Note : One bag contains approximately 50 kilograms of fertilizers.

fertilizers on a large farm is more than six times than that of a small farm. Fertilizers are invariably applied by all the big farmers almost to all the main crops. The fertilizer consumption in the village could be more but for the shortage of assured and effective irrigation facilities over large tract of the cultivated area. Since assured water supply is the pre-condition for the application of fertilizers, so it tends to act as a hindrance to their higher and wider consumption in the village. Some farmers are also averse to the use of fertilizers, as according to them, these affect adversely the natural fertility of land. But almost in the same breath they agreed that the land in the village does not respond at all without some minimum application of fertilizer.

Due to the sharp increase in the price of fertilizers and their bad effects, the farmers in the village think seriously to use campost manures instead. Manure occupies very important place in raising agriculture produce in the village. Manuring for crops is essential. For instance, manuring for sugarcane is like ritual and is done invariably by all the sugarcane growing farmers. In order to prevent exhaustion of the soil, a farmer must contantly manure it. The most common form of manure in use is cow-dung collected in a pit on the periphery of the village. The manure availability depends on the number of animals owned and also on the extent of use of cow dung as fuel for cooking purposes. The use of manure per average cultivator comes around 10.3 carts. It is 7.2 carts,

11.0 carts and 28 carts for small, medium and large cultivators respectively. Some bigger farmers also buy manure from other farmers and also the Scheduled Caste families who own sheep, goats, etc. Sometimes, they buy it even from the dairies at Rohtak.

Despite the importance of manuring, it is not collected properly in the village. According to our rough estimate, over one-fourth cow-dung is not collected and goes waste. Pits to cow-dung are not properly dug and looked after. During the rainy season, it is a common sight that cow dung gets collected on the outskirts of the village which flows freely to the low lying areas ultimately finding its way to the village pond. Surprisingly, villagers do not do anything seriously to check this menace. Also, the cattle urine which has valuable manurial properties is completely wasted. If cattle urine can be collected and mixed with cow-dung, the availability of manure will increase atleast by 10 per cent. This, however, would require serious and concerted efforts. The provision of alternative fuels for cooking to the villagers will help to increase the availability of manure for the fields. The increased use of gobar gas plants will also help in making organic manure available to the cultivators in adequate quantity. But, unfortunately, there is none in the village so far. The practice of manuring by ploughing the first crop into the soil for the second crop is also not very popular among the farmers. The methods of manuring preparations need to be taught to the farmers. All these efforts would go a long way in reducing the dependence on chemical fertilizers which has become a very costly input these days.

Insecticides : The use of insecticides as a measure to control insects and pests is made only by a few farmers in the village. The block office also supplies some plant protection chemicals but it is quite discriminatory and inadequate. Crop like Sarson is usually attacked by fungus and lacteal disease which at times wipes out the standing crop completely. There were two sprayers in Ladhot, one was with the VLM, and the other with a farmer who bought it at a subsidised price from Rohtak in 1980.

It is clear from the foregoing analysis of the usage of

techniques and inputs that people in the village, by and large, are receptive to technological changes. There is reasonable level of adoption of new technology which tends to enhance production of various crops. But further improvements can be possible provided there are more effective extension services. This would bring the knowledge of better practices at the door-steps to a wider range of farmers. We can surely endorse the basis of the findings that not enough efforts have gone into making such services effective in the village. Extension works, acceptedly, is full of difficulties which requires local participation for its success. Local participation has to be ensured by proper approach to people and by demonstrations of benefits of selected technologies. Local leadership has to be built up, demonstrations have to be given and all difficulties which people experience have to be understood and ameliorated. Without full local participation, the extension work becomes very difficult, and ultimately, the technologies may not succeed as hoped. To repeat it, it can be concluded that no substantial and serious agricultural extension work giving real attention to the problems of small-scale and poorly educated farmers has hardly begun in Ladhot. This has not happened despite the village's proximity to the block and district head-quarters.

Land Management

It is understandable that due to constant and intensive cropping, year after year, land nutrients deteriorate. The deterioration may be very rapid if nutrient to the soil is not returned by way of manures and proper crop husbandry. The problem of soil exhaustion and deterioration is also accompanied by the problem of soil erosion. Soil erosion occurs when the surface soil is washed away through floods and excessive rains. There is also the problem of salt-effervescence and water logging in the village. It is estimated that nearly five per cent of the village land has been rendered useless due to salt-effervescence alone. This serious situation warrants the farmers to introduce some kind of land management measures to their lands. The measures consist of contour bunding, bench terracing, land levelling and shaping, as well as, improved agronomical practices on agricultural lands. Soil and water conservation programmes constitute an important activity to protect the soil resources of the village in checking soil erosion and land degradation.

Land, by and large, is not managed well in the village. Many cultivators allow their land to become less fertile and barren due to mere ignorance. We found several farmers removing the fertile top soil of their land and putting it in heaps in the passage and side ways in the name of levelling their fields. Some farmers also mix in this process the salt effervescence soil with the good soil turning the later also into the former kind. Similarly, waterlogged land along the banks of mighty canal JLN, is not reclaimed properly. This land, with some additional efforts can be used for fish cultivation and growing of *singharas*. Similarly, not even a single farmer from the village ever tried to treat salt-affecting land by applying gypsum. On the basis of the facts obtained, it came to light that hardly one-fifth cultivators introduced one or the other kind of land management technique to their lands, while the remaining four-fifths had not taken to any improvement on the land for the last several years.

It becomes clear from the Table 5.4 that Jats with 24 per cent of them having introduced some land management have an edge over other caste cultivators. It is encouraging to find that the number of farmers who wish to introduce land management is almost double the number of farmers who have actually introduced it on their farms. The reasons for non-introduction of land management techniques as given by the cultivators lie, in that order of ranking, in the non-availability of expert advice, inadequacy of funds and also the absentee land ownership. The reason for non-introduction of land management can also be traced to the sheer lethargic attitude of farmers who do not feel like making any concerted efforts to reclaim the difficult and waste portion of their lands. This is particularly in case of large farmers. Also, some farmers who intend to sell their lands, sooner or later, do not feel interested in improving the quality of their lands. It may be mentioned in this context that selling of land these days is not considered disgraceful as it was twenty/thirty years back. Some farmers in the village have reported land transactions. Far-

TABLE 5.4

Land Management

Caste	Farmers Introducing Land Management		Farmers Who Wish to Introduce Land Management		Farmers Reporting Sufficiet Land		Farmers Rreporting Salea or Purchase of Land		Farmers who Dvocate Shifting Cropping Battern	
Brahmin	3	(10)	8	(28)	25	(86)	21	(72)	19	(66)
Jat	37	(24)	70	(46)	90	(59)	85	(56)	72	(47)
Saini	2	(7)	10	(34)	2	(7)	20	(69)	4	(14)
Total	42	(20)	88	(41)	117	(55)	126	(60)	95	(45.0)

Note : Figures in parenthises denote percentage to land owning

mers do also have in mind to shift the existing cropping pattern as a measure to improve land productivity. But shifting the cropping pattern is not quite an easy task as it is largely conditioned by the economic and natural factors. In all there yet exists some scope to improve land fertility by adopting suitable and appropriate cropping pattern. Land management is also possible through controlled fertilizer application and water management.

Five Year Plans

Planning for development in India has been pursued over the last 40 years with varied objectives, priorities and strategies to achieve rural growth with social justice. But the major sin, that planning has consciously or unconsciously contributed for the continued rural poverty in India, is apparent in the very nature of econometric models pursued for promoting economic growth from the very First Five Year Plan. Hence, the models, which provided the framework for the process of development, lacked in providing a suitable linkage between the macro and the micro-level activities and through details in project formulation and implementation. In fact, the link between planning at the macro-level and the projects at the micro or at the village level continued to be weak. Another important sin which is discernible from the plan documents is the lack of adequate investment in human resources in rural areas.

Micro-level planning which has moved at block level is useful and relevant. It would stimulate local people's participation and co-operative self-help. Micro-level planning, in fact, calls for an overall strategy for the development of the locality in the context of national and state goals and socio-economic objectives. Macro level planning, about which people are not fully aware, has not done much good to the village people.

It is surprising to note from Table 5.5 that even after 38 years of planning in the country, only 37 per cent of the respondents had heard about the Five Year Plans. However, there were significant variations as between different categories of households in this regard. It was relatively high in case of

TABLE 5.5

Plan Consciousness

Caste	Heard about Five Year Plans		If Yes, Do Kyou now the Present Plan Period	
	Households	Percentages	Households	Percentages
Ahir	1	33	0	0
Brahmin	10	32	1	10
Jat	50	33	4	8
Saini	12	36	1	8
Baniya	1	100	0	0
Punjabi	1	100	0	0
Khati	3	38	0	0
Kumhar	3	43	0	0
Lohar	5	38	0	0
Nai	2	67	0	0
Sonar	2	67	0	0
Bairagi	4	57	0	0
Doom	6	46	0	0
Chamar	20	44	1	5
Balmiki	18	36	0	00
Total	138	37	7	5

Punjabi, Bania and Sonar and the castes which were least informed are Ahir, Brahmin and Jat. It was equally surprising that hardly seven respondents in the entire village could tell correctly the timings and duration of the present Seventh Plan. A large number of respondents expressed the view that plans in the country had, by and large, failed to make any significant dent on rural life. This condemnation of the plans came from all the castes and also from the rich as well as poor alike.

On the basis of the above observations, it needs to be emphasised that planning should start from the village level with full participation of the villagers. Indeed, macro planning has little scope for its success. This exercise will generate a new experience and self-confidence among the village people. This does not rule out assistance from outside, but the capacity of the village community to grow from within should be the first consideration. Voluntary agencies have an important role to play in this sphere.

Communication and Urban Contacts

Outside communication and urban contacts play an important role in the growth of the village economy. Alternatively stated, economic well-being of the village is associated with the growth of communication and urbanization. We have already discussed in details the communication facilities available to the villagers in Chapter 2. It would now be our intent to know as to what extent the villagers are exposed to these means of communication.

Table 5.6 reveals that villagers make use of various means of communication viz., newspaper, radio, T.V., government agencies, neighbours, friends and relatives. It is evident that radio lures the masses and the villagers are more exposed to radio than to newspaper. The percentage of respondents who read newspapers in the village is 8.4 although there is only one person named Dharampal who subscribes to newspaper regularly. Many more villagers expressed their desire to read newspapers but they could not do that for want of library facilities in the village. Radio listening has become quite popular. About 43 per cent villagers enjoy radio listening regularly through their personal radio-sets. The most popular programme with the listeners is 'Dehati Programme' which is relayed three times a day. Radio, however, is not found much effective in disseminating knowledge in the village. It was mostly used for the purpose of entertainment. More than 75 per cent of those who listen radio confined only to 'Vivid Bharti' and 'Dehati Programme' of songs. Other useful programmes relating to agriculture etc. are not preferred by the farmers.

The villagers have also developed fancy for cinema as the traditional recreative activities like Drama, Swang, Bhajan are becoming obsolete. It was in the year 1985 that Swang or Bhajan was staged last in the village. Cinema halls in Rohtak city are thronged by the young village generation whenever a new film, particularly Haryanvi film, is screened. Last year, *Chandrawal*, a Haryanvi film, acquired a tremendous popul-

TABLE 5.6

Level of Communication and Urban Contact of the Households

	Do You Subscribe Newspaper	Do You Read the Newspaper	Do You Listen Radio Regularly	Have You Heard About T.V.	Source of Information		
					Govt. Agency	Friend, Relative	Neigh-bour
Ahir	—	—	2	3	2	3	1
Brahmin	—	9	25	31	2	3	1
Jat	1	6	60	150	3	1	2
Saini	—	3	15	30	3	2	1
Baniya	—	—	1	1	1	2	3
Punjabi	—	1	1	1	1	2	3
Khati	—	1	2	7	3	1	2
Kumhar	—	1	2	6	3	1	2
Lohar	—	1	3	11	3	2	1
Nai	—	1	3	3	1	2	3
Sonar	—	1	1	3	3	2	1
Bairagi	—	1	5	6	2	1	3
Doom	—	1	6	10	3	2	1
Chamar	—	3	20	40	2	1	3
Balmiki	—	2	15	38	3	2	1
Total	1	31	161	340	3	5	7
Percentage	0.3	8.4	43.4	91.6			

arity among the villagers due to hit songs and exalation of scene and sound. This hit film ran for several weeks at one of the Rohtak talkies. People enjoyed and carried in their memory some important events of this film for quite long. Young boys in the village memorised a few favourite film hits and hum them.

The impact of cinema on the mind of an average villager may be quite tremendous. Indeed, cinema and radio are potential sources of acquiring knowledge and can bring about attitudinal change. But their positive impact on the villagers does not appear to be very significant. There appears to be lopsided exposure to media communication, particularly cinema and radio. Cinema has created a craze among villagers to imbibe new fashions and new methods of theft and robbery. The mode of dress among the youth is also being influenced by the cinema in the village. Not only this, people in the village are now more eager to adopt the names of film stars in perference to traditional names. Cinema, undoubtedly, has a significant impact on village society. Television (T.V.) is relatively new to the villagers. There are only two T.V. sets in the village. It is a different matter that nearly all the respondents (91.6%) have heard about the T.V. machine.

While reverting to the sources of information to the villagers, it was clearly indicated that villagers acquire most of the information and knowledge from their neighbours. Friends, relatives, and government agencies in that order get only poor ranking when compared with this source The fact that neighbours are the prime source of information is indeed a good thing as the information this way can be spread to wider range of villagers. The obvious implication of this positive finding is that there is great scope to introduce and spread any useful programme quickly at a relatively low cost

Villagers' urban contacts are also important in determining their level of awareness to the new innovations, techniques and living methods. Urban contact is a potential source of acquiring knowledge and bringing attitudinal change. Urban influence on the villagers is found in evidence. The urban contacts could be possible through family members who have shifted to the urban areas and also their own purposive or casual visits to cities. The urban impact on the villagers is there but it does not appear to be very strong as it should have been in view of the vil lage being in the vicinity of Rohtak city. The urban ways in the village are gradually coming to be regarded as more respectable and progressive. The major hindrances in adopting urban ways of life occure due to illiteracy, and the self-satisfying and contended nature of the rural people. The urban impact on elderly men and women is the least. When asked about their preference for the cities, 86 per cent of them expressed their desires not, to shift to cities knowing fully the problems which they are likly to face there. Mostly, the landless educated youths, wealthy landlords and the artisans who have slender means of livelihood in the village due to the loss of their traditional professions revealed their keeness to settle in urban areas. City life certainly has some attraction but only to the rich. For the poor, shifting to the city is not less than a curse where they live in slums, and unhealthy environment and are compelled to lead a wretched existence. It may be surmised that shifting of men and material to and from the village has been important to the individual household concerned. But on the whole, it has not caused any apparent effect on the economic and social life of the village nor has it had much effect in reducing the size of the village population.

We could also guess that the relations between the rural and urban people, on the whole are not very cordial. The villagers consider urban people as cunning parasites while the urban people consider the ruralites foolish, more rustic and less civilized. One can see in cities urban shopkeepers persuading the rural people to buy the articles at exorbitant rates. If they try rates at several other places then other will also cheat them very badly. Infact, there is no one to advise the rural people to help them to escape from the fraudulent business practices of urban people. The same thing happens when the villagers go to attend the court and some other office in the city. They made complaints that there are men everywhere in the towns and cities waiting to exploit gullibility. In the courts avaricious lawyers abound, ready to offer legal advice in return for a huge fee. The affluence of lawyers and businessmen at

Rohtak in some cases is proverbial Many have thrived merely on the ignorance and helplessness of the villagers.

Health and Sanitation

General health and sanitation in the village are far from satisfactory. Although, there is a dispensary in the village but people mostly do not depend on it for treatment. It is in bad shape, even ordinary medicines are not always available. Similarly, the services of government appointed mide-wife available in the village are rarely availed of and maternity cases are attended by local untrained *dai*. No doubt, some serious diseases such as malaria and small-pox which used to take a heavy toll of life are controlled and eradicated from this village as from any other village. But the general health of the people is not sound and many individual suffer from one or the other ailment and are cachectic. This is quite evident from the sickly looks of the people. Even the school going children don't look healhty. Although, the school should arrange for medical check ups as per the provision but nobody seems to care. There must be a large number of children in the village school who would first like to be provided proper food and anything afterwards there are hardly any facilities for sports and games for children. They are also not taught about civic habits.

There is not a single public latrine or urinal in the entire village and for most of the people the nearby fields serve as unsanctioned community latrine. There is no drainage system and even a small quantity of rain makes the village lanes, particularly the kucha ones, muddy and slushy. Fortunately, a greater part of the village is situated at an elavated level and water finds a natural outlet.

Very few people keep their clothes washed and clean. They also use toilet soaps and some detergents. For heavy clothes a wooden stick called *mogra* is used for treating the clothes for washing. Clothes are also ironed and pressed —a habit limited only to the educated few and the new generation youth. The old ones and those engaged in agriculture and other manual and menial activities are not very particular about their dresses and the cleanliness of their body. Similarly, old ladies who wear a *Ghagra* measuring upto 50 metres cloth and also keep *chunda* cannot keep themselves very clean even if they are keen.

Morning hygiene with most of the villagers, is not an important matter. Daily brushing of teeth is not done by a majority of people. Tooth paste is used by only those who are in service otherwise neem or babul twigs are used for the purpose. In case of ladies, cleaning of teeth is very rare and infrequent. Because of the type of occupation which they are to perform, a morning bath is not quite possible. Bathing is generally done in the open in the evening. Ladies, as discussed in Chapter 2, take their bath at night under the cover of darkness and when they return to bed after the day's chores.

Owing to traditional motions and lack of guidance people in the village do not seem to bother much about cleanliness. The village can be made more clean with no additional cost but through some efforts and mutual cooperation among the village people. Nature in the village is bounty of which people do not seem to take advantage. We came across people of different age groups who were absorbed in playing cards and engaged in gossips over *hukka* for hours together but never thought of having morning or evening walks. A conversation with them revealed that they knew nothing about keeping fit. For them, the way to ensure health, involves consumption of more desi ghee and milk, nothing beyond.

Family Planning

There is, undisputably, a need to adopt a positive population policy in the village to restrict its growing population. The task of limiting the population can be accomplished with the help of Family Planning measures, right type of education and economic betterment of the people. Raising the level of education particularly that of the female, will have a general salutary effect on procreation. Assuming, that the Family Planning Programme is the salient feature of the national population policy, we obtained the views of the respondents in this regard. The table 5.7 contains such views.

Nearly four-fifths respondents believe that the human number in their family far exceed their resources and means. And about the same number is found willing to restrict the

TABLE 5.6

Attitude Towards Population and Family Planning

(Number)

Caste	Over Population	Need to Restrict Family	In Favour of Family Planning	Favouring 2-3 Children Per Couple	Favouring 18-21 Age at Marriage	Preference for Nuclear Family
Ahir	1	1	1	1	1	1
Brahmin	29	28	23	22	4	21
Jat	150	138	130	135	110	125
Saini	27	27	24	27	5	24
Baniya	1	1	1	1	—	1
Punjabi	1	1	1	1	—	1
Khati	1	1	1	1	—	1
Kumhar	5	5	5	5	2	3
Lohar	1	1	1	1	1	2
Nai	3	3	3	3	3	2
Sonar	3	3	3	3	2	2
Bairagi	6	6	6	6	7	6
Doom	12	12	12	12	8	7
Chamar	30	25	20	20	25	30
Balmiki	25	21	20	20	24	28
Total	295	273	251	258	192	254
Percentage	80	74	68	70	52	69

families. Most of them feel that unplanned family gives rise to varied types of economic and social problem. Of the measures adopted to restrict families. Family Planning Programme was adopted by 68 per cent of the respondents in the village and the variations among different castes are nominal. This is a welcome sign and thus there is need to adopt coercive methods for the successful implementation of the Family Planning Programme as far as this village is concerned. The misuse of power by the government during the period of emergency to meet the targets of Family Planning still haunts the minds of the people. During the emergency period, several people of the village were rounded up by the district administration for the success or mass vasectomy camps. In this process, the overzealous officers led to a distortion of the programme in various ways. It may also be pointed out that the acceptance level of Family Planning by the poor section of the society (after 3-4 children) was significantly related to the monetory incentives. We, however, could not determine exactly the couples using Family Planning methods in the village. But we guess that the number is fairly good.

Government has increasingly realised over time that Family Planning can succeed only if child survival rate is raised. So, for the achievement of the 'two child' norm, it is essential that the child survival rate is sufficiently raised. The data thrown by village survey in connection with the expressed desire to limit the number of children is quite encouraging. About 70 per cent families revealed their preference for 2-3 children and expressed that the number beyond this would give rise to all sorts of economic and social problems. In case of Scheduled Castes the number of children desired, however, is more than this number. Notably, nearly all the respondents revealed their preference for male to female children. Most of them wanted to have a combination of two sons and one daughter.

Reverting to the measures to restrict the family, raising the age of marriage is the important one. When asked about the proper age for marriage, about 52 per cent of the households preferred 18 to 22 years as the ideal age for marriage of girl and boy, respectively. A large number of persons favouring this age group is indicative of the fact that social changes, affecting the mean age at marriage, are taking place in the village and in all probability this trend would continue in future as well. It is estimated that this factor alone will contribute roughly to 10 per cent decline in conception and birth in the next coming years. If, however, the rate of literacy rises this may further help to slow down the rate of population increase in the village. The process of the breaking up of joint families into nuclear ones would help in controlling the fertility of the couples in the village. Various studies have affirmed that nuclear family system allows smaller family expansion.

This, however, is definite that unless a social consciousness about family limitation becomes more strong in the village, the creation of physical apparatus in the form of clinic, distributing free contraceptive etc. will be of no avail. It was seen that the contraceptive *Nirodh* was used by the village children as a baloon for their game and fun. The motivation for limitting the family is a crucial factor. This, however, will require the transformation of social and psychological attitudes which will come about with high literacy, high urban contacts and the economic well-being.

Politics

As in case of any village, Local politics affects people in Ladhot village. The on going politics becomes more active and brisk particularly during election time may it be Panchayat election, State Assembly election or general Parliamentary elections. The people get split on political lines. The split among castes and households during Panchayt election, is not the same as during Assembly or Parliamentary elections. In the case of Panchayat elections the main division is within castes while it is between castes in Assembly or Parliamentary elections. However, there had been no politically motivated serious untoward incident in the village during all these elections. There is also not much in evidence when any politician of the area put one group of persons against another group in the village although groupism and a detrioration in inter-personal relations cannot be denied.

Political consciousness has increased manifold over the

TABLE 5.8

Political Consciousness

Caste	Do you know some political party	Are you member of any political party	Households: Your preference for the political party due to		
			Leader	Performance	Tradition
Ahir	3	—	1	2	3
Brahman	31	2	2	3	1
Jat	153	20	1	2	3
Saini	33	2	1	2	3
Baniya	1	—	1	2	3
Punjabi	1	—	2	3	1
Khati	8	—	1	3	2
Kumhar	7	—	2	1	3
Lohar	13	—	2	3	1
Nai	3	—	1	2	3
Sonar	3	—	3	2	1
Bairagi	7	—	1	3	2
Doom	13	—	2	1	3
Chamar	45	3	2	3	1
Balmiki	50	2	2	3	1
Total	371	29	7	2	6

years since independence. They take interest in politics and also discuss political leaders. They are aware of the political decisions and political upheavals in the state, nay, in the country. The head-man and some other persons do have links with local administration and politicians. But there is nothing in the memory of the villagers when any politician or local M.L.A. was called upon to adjudicate in disputes over land oı other matters in the village. National politics, as indicated earlier, interests the villagers but not as deeply as local or state politics. The local power structure, although, originally so strongly pro-Congress yet during the last several years a majority of people of Ladhot have been voting for the Lok Dal Party (Now JantaDal) co-terminous with the 1987 Assembly elections. Table 5.8 would also give some added information regarding the form of politics in the village.

The level of political consciousness among the villagers is quite high. All the respondents could easily name one or more political party in the country. The political parties which they named of course, in most of the cases, were confined to the Lok Dal and the Congress (I). There is no third political party in the vlllage which carries any force. Despite this high level of consciousness, there are only 29 active members belonging to different political parties, in the whole village. When asked about the reason for their preference for a political party, three important reasons viz. leadership, performance and tradition came to be listed. Preference for leader was found to be the deciding factor in 7 out of 15 castes. Surprisingly, performance is found to be the least important factor governing the voter's chocie of party or leader. In case of last Haryana State Assemble elections held in May 1987, the preference was clearly for the leader, and people over-whelmingly voted for the Lok Dal (B) on account of this factor. Of the 966 votes polled in the village in this election, Lok Dal (B) secured 599 votes which comes to about 62 per cent of the votes polled.

CHAPTER 6

SUMMARY AND CONCLUSIONS

This chapter summarizes the main findings and provides some broad conclusions of the study revealed through investigation. Ladhot is an ancient village with a rich past. It is situated about eight kilometres in the north-east of Rohtak city. The village is multicaste having as many as 15 castes. According to the survey year 1985, the village possesses 671 hectares of land area, 371 households and a population of 2372 individuals. The rate of population in Ladhot, though tending to slow down is still high. There are sufficient indications that it will drop in future largely due to two crucial reasons. First, people are not averse to the idea of family planning and a majority of couples revealed their preference only upto two or three children. It is, however, another matter that most of them showed their preference for sons over daughters. Second, the emerging trend of nuclear family which normally does not allow any vast expansion, would also help in controlling the procreative dimensions of couples in the village.

Education is a necessary concomitant to the changing ideology and culture of the community. The level of literacy which is uneven among different castes, has registered an increase in the village over the time period. There appears greater awakening among parents and guardians to impart better and high education to their children. Indeed, the social demand for education is constantly increasing in the village.

According to the villagers, education is an important entry ticket for getting good jobs and also improves matrimonial prospects. Education for girls is not considered superflous now. However, schooling in the village still bristles with several problems which need to be solved. For example, teachers' apathy towards students in both the schools in the village craves remedial measures at various levels. Most of the teachers come from outside and don't feel involved in the process of character-making. Naturally, students depend heavily on unfair means to pass their examinations. It is a crying need that teachers pay greater attention to everything concerning the educative process. They must learn to love village life. Besides inadequacy at the level of educators, the facilities in the village schools are far from satisfactory. Owing to these and many other reasons some students, whose parents can afford, go to Rohtak and other towns for better schooling.

Agricultural development is *sine-qua-non* for the growth of the village economy. Distribution of agricultural land and its allocation to individual crops play a strategic role in the growth of village agriculture. The land in the village is not only scarce but also there is little scope on its extensive margin. However, efforts can be made to reclaim and check water-logged and salt-affected land which is an ever-growing menace. All this requires concerted land management efforts which, unfortunately, are not in much evidence among the farmers. Land, which is the main source of livelihood in the village, is unequally distributed among the households. About two-fifths of the total households from nine castes do not own any land. Those who own it, the average size of the holding works out only 2.8 hectares. There is preponderance of small holdings which measure 2 hectares or less in size. All such holdings account for more than three-fifths of the total holdings in the village. Not only the holdings are small but they are also badly fragmented due to the sub-division of landed property among joint owners, each of whom wants a share in each quality of ancestral land. In this process, the gains of consolidation of holdings tend to neutralize. At present, the number of economically viable holdings in the village is very small. In fact, there exists no scope at all to acquire land, under the provision of ceiling, which can be distributed among the landless and marginal cultivators who have a hunger for land.

Tenancy is extensively prevalent in the village as more than half of the total agricultural land is involved in it. Contrary to the belief generally held, small farmers turn out to be net leasors-out and large-sized farmers are found leasing in land substantially. The leasing-in the land by the small farmers is inter alia, due to the derive to make the full use of the fixed farm resources particularly the family labour and draft power which is abundanec in supply with them. Some important features land tenancy which are observed in the village are : Farmers tend to lease out the worst part of their land which generally is also located at a sufficient distance from the village ; land is fequently leased to brother or other close friend for fear of tenancy law ; tenancy is without any record and is rotated among different tenants after a year or two ; and tenancy in the village takes two forms viz share cropping and some fixed annual rent with cost sharing. The above revealing features of tenancy are at once good and bad. Despite the often cited demerits of tenancy, it does give something to the landlord, tenant, or both which is not easily achieved by any other alternative arrangement.

Allocation of agricultural land among different competing crops is vital and crucial in the wake of scarcity of land. The land allocation decision will reflect the resources under the control of the household, the quality and suitability of land, amount of family labour, draft and tractor power and also aversion or willingness to undertake risk. The cropping pattern in the village is not of monoculture or twinculture type but is quite diversified where as many as 17 crops are raised during Kharif and Rabi seasons. Land use is heavily biased towards food crops. Wheat alone accounts for 60 per cent of the cropped area due mainly to the successful adoption of HYV seed. A sharp decline in area under gram, sugarcane and near non-existent area under fruit and vegetables is a matter of great concern. The general attitude of the people in this regards needs to be researched. The cropping pattern in the absence of these crops and remedied vastly accounts for the poor health of the people for whom the sources of physical energy (calorie and protein) are only cereals and sugar. More recently, farmers have experienced that wheat no longer is a remunerative crop due to the sharp rise in the cost of cultivation. But the farmers do not keep accounts and they go on cultivating wheat traditionally despite the decline in its profitability. There is a need to squeeze the area under wheat and divert it to other crops such as gram, sugarcane, vegetables and oil-seeds.

The overall intensity of cropping which fluctuates around 170 can be considered high. But this can be pushed up further if the irrigation facilities are augmented. It is a matter of great concern that some crops get wasted partially or wholly due to drought, flood, inclement weather and disease. The crop loss exceeded 26 per cent of the total cropped area in the village in 1983. In case of individual crops, the loss sometimes is complete and total and the consequences of crop failure are extremely severe if not catastrophic. This comes as a back breaking experience for the cultivators. In view of the above record of crop failure, due the reasons beyond the control of the farmers, there is a strong case for crop insurance. The crop insurance would go a long way in stabilizing agriculture in the village. Actually, no sustained and steady development of agricultural economy is possible without some form of crop insurance to underwrite the risk of crop failure. This is high time that the State government give a serious thought to this proposal and make it a workable proposition.

Like land there is also skewed distribution in respect of the non-land assets of the village. Assets distribution and housing facilities in the village reveal and affirm that there are widespread differences in these among different castes. Houses. mostly, are pucca, constructed with brick and mortar. These are also 38 kucha houses made from mud brick, and these mostly belong to the Scheduled Caste families. Obviously, these houses are much inferior, less commodious and less elegant. Regarding the household durables of luxury items such as scooter, fan, television, sofa-sets, these are concentrated among higher caste families of Brahmins and Jats. Wrist-watch, cycles, tape-recorder are catching the fancy of the villagers and are equally popular among all castes including the Scheduled Castes. But, on the whole, the Scheduled Castes and other poor families are characterized by poor assets values due to the low and inferior quality of these assets.

The availability of farm implements vastly reflects the level of involvement of households in agriculture. It is observed that indigenous tools are gradually being replaced by the improved tools of cultivation. At present there are 28 tractors, 36 tubewells and 36 wheat threshers in the village—a situation which gives credence to the view that agriculture in the village is reasonably mechanised. Regarding the livestock wealth, there are varied types of animals in the village kept for different purposes. He-buffalo is replacing the bullock as the former is more economical and more convenient for certain agricultural operations. At the same time, it has become quite difficult these days to maintain good quality bullock, on account of the shrinking of holding size and non-availability of costly gram—a diet must for their sustenance.

There exists close relationship between the growth of an economy and occupational structure. There are several occupations in the village—agriculture predominating. Generally, occupations in the village are closely related to castes and are specific and pre-determined. But there are clear evidences of drift from the traditional occupations. Many families in several castes carry out simultaneously subsidiary and of altogether new occupations alongwith their traditional ones. As indicated, agriculture is a common vocation without any caste barriers which has been taken up by several castes. As mentioned, there are indications that tendency of the households toward caste occupation is dwindling in the village and the fact of caste identification with the traditional occupations remains somewhat less identified. It is also revealed clearly that most families are dissatisfied with their caste occupation and wish for themselves and for their children to take up new and other professions available preferably in the urban areas. The desire for occupational mobility is a sign of modernization, but there are certain constraints which prevent the villagers to take up the occupations of their own choice. The important constraints are: poor and few opportunities, inadequate qualifications, attachment to land and native vlllage and obligations to the parents.

The incidence of unemployment is very heavy in this village. Unemployment and under-employment are the main economic problems of the adults in the village. The unemployment has two aspects seasonal and perennial. It has been observed that agriculture which is already burdened with under-employment and has reached the point of saturation in terms of land use and intensity of cropping can not absorb the rising labour force in the village any more. So the avenues, outside agriculture have to be found. Several educated youths in the village have spent a very long period of joblessness leading them to the point of despair and frustration. Unemployment among the poor is still more wide-spread as they do not have the right connections or the slush money for getting jobs. The various programmes launched by the government have not been successful to cope with the problem of reducing the incidence of unemployment in the village. For the successful employment policy in the village, a vigorous and meaningful policy of small industries linked with village agriculture and in consonance with the skill and resource endowments in the village should be pursued. At present, there is not a single such industry worth the name in the village. Not only this, no serious efforts are on anvil in this direction. As a lasting solution to the problem of under-employment the growth of labour should be stamped through positive population policy for which there exist understandable chances of success.

Savings are reported by only a few households which is an indication of poverty in the village. Average houschold saving to the tune of Rs. 3540 only per annum could be reckoned meagre by any standard. More than one-third saving is kept at home and the rest in banks, post-offices or invested in LIC policies. There is no bank branch in the village. If some bank branch is opened in the villlage then it can expect to mop up some savings by developing banking habits among the villagers, especially the cultivators, Scheduled Castes and illiterates who are yet to make a real beginning in this respect.

More than one-third of the households in the village

depend upon outside finance to meet their pressing financial requirements. The amount of borrowing varies considerably between castes. Borrowing has become more or less inevitable to a larger proportion of cultivators to carry out their agricultural operations. Over 16 per cent of the households reported borrowing from money lenders, more than 20 per cent from friends and relatives, more than 36 per cent from the Land Development Bank and over 12 per cent from other agencies. Borrowing from Land Development Bank figures prominently in the overall borrowing structure of the village. In fact, it was this loan that enabled the farmers to go in for the tractors, tubewells and other agricultural implements in the village, though farmers encountered some difficulties in obtaining and availing this loan. Repayment of loans to the bank is the major and constant source of worry to the farmers. The decision of the State government to waive-off some part of the loans would ease out, to some extent, the hardships of the loanees in Ladhot village as elsewhere in the State. The co-operative loan in the village is nil as the co-operative credit society was wound up long back due to its malfunctioning. It was also noticed on collating that a significant share of the borrowed loans was spent, by many, for purposes other than for which those were made.

Market facilities both for varied kind of inputs and outputs is a major requirement in the development of village economy. Labour market in the village is provided, mostly, by the landless families and is adequate despite the fluctuations in demand due to seasonal variations. During lean agricultural seasons, village labour is hired outside the village in the city. There is hardly any intra-village transaction of labour. Labour is hired on cash and wage contract, and also on share contract in case of crop harvesting under which one-twentieth share of the crop harvested goes to the labour. Sometimes, labour is also provided meals in addition to cash settled, but now this practice has become quite rare in the village. Interestingly, high caste do not hire out their services as labour in the village their poor economic conditions notwithstanding. The practice of bullock hiring in the village is quite uncommon. Tractor hiring services, on the other hand, are easily available on request. Market for credit consists of several sources which provided credit on different terms and conditions. There is no seed store and fertilizer depot in the village. However, farmers have good knowledge as to where these two inputs might be available in the city. Canal water is the main source of irrigation and is not sold out, though mutual exchange of water is generally made to make it better and more effective. However, a few tube-well owners sell their water to their neighbouring farmers. Agricultural produce in the village is largely sold out in the city market, though some produce is also disposed off locally to the needy households in the village itself. The surplus produce of wheat and sugarcane is taken to Rohtak. Wheat sometimes is sold in Narela grain market in Delhi Union Territory, where the prices tend to relatively high. The wheat straw is sold in the village and is also stacked by the farmers for use during lean months. The arrangement for selling sugarcane to the co-operative mills located at Rohtak, is not convenient and mill is also accused of paying delayed payments for the cane delivered. Milk is also sold in the city by some eight milkmen who collect milk from various households in the village. For other small requirements of goods and services, there are ten odd shops scattered in the village which cater to the day-to day requirements of the households. The solitary fair price shop in the village does not work efficiently and regularly. To meet other various requirements of cloth, agricultural accessories, furniture, footwear, utensils, vegetables, ghee, medicines, the village, dependrs on city markets, where it is alleged, they are fleeced badly.

The general level of nutrition and food which determines the physical and mental growth of population is poor in the village. It is observed that the small farmers and landless labourers and their children do not get wholesome food and are hungriest of all and suffer from mal-nutrition. Importantly, malnutrition among the rich is not due to scarcity of good food but wrong food choices and bad habits coupled with ignorance. The staple food of the entire village is wheat and bajra loaves. These are taken day in and day out with monotonous regularity. The general cambination with bread is dal, some vegetables, jaggery, onion, lassi, tea and sauce. Per capita consumption of milk, ghee, mustard oil, gram, sugar, gur is deplorable, with some exceptions. Substantial quantity of the milk produced in the village is sold out in the city. Tea is replacing milk and lassi. Indeed, the near disappearance of gur and gram is the most alarming of the many changes in the diet of the villagers. Two decade ago, any villager could have these two things, but now these are getting beyond the reach of the common man. It is beyond doubt that the diet of the majority of people is unbalanced and there is no conspicuous place for fruit and vegetables. Things become worse for those who drink and smoke heavily and there is no dearth of such persons in the village.

Despite the facility of dispensary in the village, the general health of the people is not sound. There are many persons who suffer from one or other ailment and are cachetic. The dispensary in the village is in bad shape. The health of the majority of schoolgoing children who bear famished looks, is not sound. There must be a large number of children in the village schools who would first like to eat more and then do anything else. There are no public latrines or urinals. Similarly, no proper water channels exist and even a small quantity of rain makes the villege lanes particularly the *kucha* ones muddy and slushy. Morning hygiene is not an important matter with a majority of the people. People are ignorant about the simple ways and techniques to keep fit. People do not give much importance to bath room and kitchen facilities while designing construction for their houses. Smokeless chulah which is free from the defect of traditional chulah, surprisingly, has not found favoure with the women-folk. In many cases of households, who do not own separate cattle sheds, inmates of the house and cattle share the common roof which is quite unhygienic. Similarly, compost pits and dung heaps are not properly kept, and the contents are washed away in rains into the village ponds. Interestingly these ponds serve the water needs of the cattle in the village all the year round making them susceptible to numerous diseases and resultant deformities.

The relations among different castes in the village can be

termed cordial. However, there are some inhibitions which hinder the process of interaction among castes on the celebration of marriage and other social functions. Broadly seen, such inhibitions are now quite on the wane. Nearly 60 per cent of the households believe in caste identity. But the educated ones and those who are in service have cultivated liberal attitudes. There is perfect harmony in community living. The village has large number of families from different castes where people commonly share their pleasures and pains and joys and sorrows. But surprisingly enough, Chamar and Balmiki the two Scheduled Castes maintain distance and keep segregation with each other. Balmiki is the caste despised most in the village. The rivalry between Brahmins and Jats which sometimes becomes apparent during election time is short lived. The institution of caste is inimical to the free flows and exchange of ideas. But it is happy to note that barriers to castes are breaking down though gradually. This is owing to such of the multiple factors as modernization, industrialization, urbanization, democracy and education which tend to strike at the very root of the caste system. Villagers now care little to the traditionally defined or demarcated positions-superior and inferior of various castes. Some lower castes have adopted the customs, manners and even titles and surnames of upper castes without inviting any criticism and effective opposition from the latter. But a majority of upper castes is still not in favour of continuation of the granting of several concessions by the government to Backward and Scheduled Castes.

Marriages are performed mostly during the months of May and June after the harvesting of wheat is over. This is owing to the fact that marriage expenses are generally met out of the sale proceeds of wheat—a major cash crop. Marriages take place within one's own caste but not within the same sub-caste or lineage. This poses a very serious problem for the villagers in the matter of selecting a suitable match. The marriages, by and large, are arranged, i.e., selection of mates are made by the parents rather than by the partners themselves. Child marriage has become quite uncommon even with the Scheduled Castes. Marital alliances, to the extent possible, are restricted to a smaller geographical expanse. Dowry system has come to stay in the village. But it is mostly voluntary and not out of duress and coercion. Such examples are very rare where land or any other valuable asset was sold or mortgaged to pay for dowry. Views condemning dowry are expressed by all but sadly it is not put to practice by many.

Panchayat of hereditary leaders or caste panchayat has not much of role to play in the village. On the contrary, the statutory village Panchayat wields authority and power over the entire village. All major castes in the village have representation in the existing Panchayat body. Most of the members are uneducated and ordinary villagers and thus have not much of vision and planning for the growth of the village. The Panchayat, no doubt, has undertaken some development activities in the village but it does not evince any interest to propagate and help the various government plans meant for the villagers. The financial limitation has been the major bane of the Panchayat resulting in a limited success in attaining the objectives. Factionalism in the village is yet another snag which has also contributed to its partial failure and has limited its role in the socio-economic upliftment of the village.

Festivals play a significant role in the village life. The important festivals celebrated in the village include Holi, Dussehra, Diwali, Rakhi, Teej, Krishanasthami, Kanagat, Maker Sankaranti and Shivaratri. Most of these festivals are jointly celebrated by all communities without any caste distinc tion. Besides the celebration of these festivals, there is an occasional staging of Bhajan, Swang and Ramlila in the village. The village life, excepting these occasions, remains quite dull. The sources of entertainment are near non-existent. In order to break the monotony of village people a video centre can be set up. But the shows should be regulated in such a manner that films glamourising sex, violence, vulgarity and brutality are not shown.

The government has been launching several programmes from times to time to ameliorate the lot of the people in the village. But most of there could not be successful either due to poor implementation or poor participation of the people or both. For instance, land ceiling as an important measure of land reform could not be implemented in the village, inter-alia,due to some loopholes in the ceiling laws. The ceiling laws were watered down in the process of implementation. The farming community with the exception of marginal farmers, did not favour the ceiling laws and argued that land if transferred to the landless will result in dissipating the resources deployed in village agriculture, and would also lead to serious social tension in the village. Similarly other programmes under the banner of community development and other popular programmes mostly remained on papers and their impact on village community is not much visible. Whatever, little benefits these programmes had these accrued only to the influential and rich persons. As such these programmes leave much to be desired and efforts should be made so that percolation effects of these programmes become more significant in the village. People in the village are not found in favour of co-operative movement in its any shape and form. Their experience with the co-operative society which would up owing to its malfunctioning had left a bitter taste in their mouths.

Fortunately, farmers in the village are not bound by contention and outmoded traditions. Many of them are ready to accept technical changes. Tradition does not appear to be a serious hindrance in the modernisation of agriculture. The farmers showed distinct change in the matter of adoption of High Yielding Varieties Programmes, usage of fertilizers and other improved methods of cultivation. It may be surmised, farmers are receptive to technical change, whenever such opportunities are offered to them. There, however, is noticed great variation across farmers in this behalf. There are farmers who are more alert to opportunities and also less alert and less receptive. The latter category of farmers seems to plod along from day to day and year to year without much botheration in the analysis of their decisions.

The consciousness of the village people in respect of various vital programmes going on in the state and the country is quite low. It was distressing to note that even after 40 years of planning, only 37 per cent of the village respondents had heard about the Five Year Plans. This points to the lack of plan consciousness among the people. Hardly seven per cent respondents could tell correctly about the on-going Seventh Five

Year Plan period. This re-inforces the view that the failure of plans is due to non-involvement of the common man in the planning process. Actually, planning should start from the village level with full participation of the villagers. Micro level planning will generate a new experience and self-confidence among the village people. The district level planning has come to stay. But the science of its formulation and the art of its implementation is not wholly in order and thus needs to be improved for its suceess.

Outside communication and urban contacts play an importan role in the growth of the village economy and the mode of living in the village. The study reveals that the village people maintain several linkages with the outside world. Such links are established through communication (rail, road) and several other means like newspaper, radio, television, friends and relatives. Due to the influence of these means there is some change in the values and attitudes of the people. The change, however, is not a significant as it should have been in view of the proximity of the village to Rohtak city which is a business and commercial centre and also fairly advanced in other spheres as well. Several respondents opined that the urban contacts have led to the development of individualistic, selfish and separatist tendencies among them. And the glamour of village life in respect of corporate unity, functional inter-dependence of various castes is decaying rapidly. They further allege that the serenity of old rural society is disappearing and life now is full of tension due to urban contacts.

It also came to light that migration from the village to city has taken place from cross-section of the population but it tends to be more strong among the more intelligent, the educated and the well-to-do. And if this movement steadily continues, the village population will tend to become less virile and more inert. Another negative feature of the migration has been that it has given rise to conflict, invariably, in all families between the serving members and the members who stay behind in village and are engaged in agriculture or other related activities. The mistrust and dispute in most cases in such joint families arises due to the non-furnishing of accounts of their income by both sides.

People are becoming politically aware and can appreciate how politics affects them in the village. The ongoing politics becomes more active and brisk particularly during elections. People now discuss more often the politics and political leaders. Though local politics is the main focus for them but they also discuss the national politics and issues involved in it. No doubt, the Jats are numerically and economically the strongest but the distribution of political power and authority in Ladhot does not show any correlation between the two. Certainly, castes have lately been used by the politicians as factors influencing the electorate but the recent Assembly Elections in Haryana (May 1987) has falsified this belief. Now the village people cannot be taken for granted as they are not always swayed by caste consideration alone.

From the foregoing discussion it is clear that village is in the process of modernization though the change is not as rapid as it should have been. There is also noticed a desire to preserve the village traditions. The improved means of communication, proximity of urban centres, two schools, medical dispensary, veterinary hospital, postal facilities, availability of good potable underground water, a good number of tractors and other improved farm implements are the important factors that are indicative of change in the village. People are receptive to technological changes and are conscious about their inter-relationship with the wider economic social and political system. But some changes in the village have also introduced conflict and tension in the minds of the people.

It is also brought out significantly that rural poverty and inequality is much in evidence in the village. Despite some development and changes, people are facing a ruinous prospect particularly in those households which are solely dependent on agriculture and allied activities. The terms of trade which remained systematically loaded against the farmers and other villagers have further eroded their income and worsened the situation for them. We all accept the simple fact that rural population must be reasonably prosperous to provide the requisite purchasing power for absorbing the products of modern industry.

Poverty and other problems are not impossible to eradicate

provided there is a political will and commitment to realistic policies oriented to the development needs of the villagers. It has become almost an imperative that the villagers must organise themselves so as to influence the policies and programmes framed for them. Actual involvement of common man in the village in the process of planning is essential. Corrective and remedial measures should be initiated immediately in certain fields. Education in the village must improve ; surplus labour should be absorbed in non-agricultural activities, something must be done to arrest further sub-division and fragmentation of land holdings ; people should desist from wrong habits of heavy drinking and smoking; and educated individuals should take living interest in the welfare of their village. Only then substantial and desired improvement in the economic and social conditions of the village may be possible.

APPENDIX 'A'

QUESTIONNAIRE

SOCIO-ECONOMIC STATUS OF AN INDIAN VILLAGE
DEPARTMENT OF COMMERCE, M.D. UNIVERSITY, ROHTAK

Name of the Head of the Family :____________________.

Name of the Respondent : ____________________.

Main Occupation :____________________.

Subsidiary Occupation :____________________.

Caste :____________________.

Religion : ____________________.

Family—

Type of the Family Joint Nuclear Single

Family Size	Male		Female		Total	
	Adult	Minor	Adult	Minor	Adult	Minor

Household Assets

Asset	Number	Model/ Brand	When Acquired	Current Market Value (Rs.)
Scoo ter				
Cyc le				

Sewing Machine
Fan Table/Ceiling
Furniture
(a) Chair
(b) Table
(c) Sofa-Set
(d) Other
Radio-set
T.V.- Set
Tape-Recorder
Watch
Utensils
(a) Brass
(b) Stainless Steel
(c) Other Metal
Heater Gadget
Suitcase
Dresses
Pair of Shoes
Cot/Dewan
Double bed
Any Other
Cattle/Animal

I. Draft Animals	Number	Present Market Value (Rs.)
Bullock		
Camel		
He-buffalo		

II. Milch Cattle	Number	Milk Yield	Present Market Value (Rs.)
Buffalo			
Cow Desi			
Cow Jersey			

III. Young Stock	Number	Present Market Value (Rs.)

IV. Other Animals	Number	Present Market Value (Rs.)
Goat		
Horse		
Donkey		
Mule		
Pig		
Sheep		
V. Poultry Birds		

Total Savings (Cash)

	Amount (Rs.)
Bank	
Post-Office	
Home	
L.I.C.	
Lending	
Other	

Borrowings	Amount	When	Acquired	Purpose	Defaulter	Rate of Interest	Your Experience
Govt. Agency							
Cooperative Societies							
Land Development Bank							
Money Lender							
Bank							
Relative							
Friend							
Other							

Marketing of Produce/Product

Product	Market	Rate	When Sold	When Bought	Quantity
1					
2					
3					
4					
5					
6					
7					
8					
9					
10					

Marketing Problems, Experiences in Order of Ranking

(i) Low price
(ii) Distress Sale
(iii) Transportation
(iv) Malpractices
(v) Any other

Living Conditions

No.	Houses	Area Metres	Kucha	Pucca	Rooms	Kitchen	Toilet	Bath room	Electricity Consumption
1.									
2.									
3.									

Cattle-Shed
Number
Separate or Not
Pucca/Kucha
Use of Cattle-Shed

Milk and oil Products

Milk Production Daily (Lts.)	Consumption (Lts.)	Marketed (Lts.)

Ghee consumption per month in Kgs.

Vegetable Ghee consumption per month in kg.

Mustard oil consumption per annum in kgs.

Sugar consumption per month in kgs.

Gur and Shakar per month in kgs.

Preparation of Vegetable daily or not

ECUCATION, LEVEL OF EMPLOYMENT

Name :

Age.

Male/Female

Education

Year of Completion of Education.

Married/Unmarried

Employed/Unemployed/Underemployed

Job/Occupation

Income

Salary p.m.

Place of Working

Distance

Remittance To Family

Job Satisfaction Yes/No

Job Preference

Daily Passenger
or Not
Land Holding (Acres/Hectares)
    Owned
    Leased-in
    Leased-out
    Total Operated
Number of fragments of Land ________________
Fragments before consolidation ________________
Size of each fragment
Distance of fragment from village
Land unfit for Cultivation
Land Transaction
    Reasons for selling
    Rate
    Where
    Area
    Purchased
    Rate
    Where

Irrigation	Land Irrigated (Hectare)	Frequency of Irrigation	Non-irrigated (Hectare)
(a) Canal			
(b) Tubewell			
(c) Well/Persian Wheel			
(d) Other			

Cropping Pattern

Crop	Hectares	Irrigated/ Unirrigated	Variety HYV/ Traditional	Yield Total	Yield per Hectare
Wheat					
Gram					

Wheat +
Gram
Barley
Paddy
Sugarcane
Mustard
Bajra
Jowar
Cotton
Toria
Vegetables
Barseem
Garden
Methi
Mator
Other

Farm Implements

Item	Number	Model/ Make	When Acquired	Present Market Value	Self-finance/ Loan
Farm House					
Tractor					
Diesel-Engine					
Tube-well					
Well					
Thresher					
Harvester					
Bar-harrow					
Disc-harrow					
Cultivators					
Seed-drill					
Cane Crusher					

Chaff Cutter
Cart Iron/Wooden
Buggi
Plough (Wooden)
Plough (Iron)
Sprayers
Duster
Flour mill
Oil Crusher
Implement Shed
Other

Agricultural Practices

Fertilizers	Type	Quantity used (Bags)	Cost	Market
1				
2				
3				

Manures
Insecticides and
Pesticides
Electricity Consumed
on Farms (units)
HYV Programme Difficulties, Give Ranking

Procurement of Seed
Procurement of Fertilizer
Water Shortage
Power Shortage
Labour Shortage
Lack of finance
Marke tin

Susceptibility to Pests
Any Other

Land Management

Is your land sufficient for you ? Yes No
Do you want to sell or purchase land and why ?
Have you introduced any land mgt. to your land ?
Do you keep an account of your business ?
What do you think about Agricultural Tax ?
Have you shifted your cropping pattern ?
Are irrigation facilities adequate ?
How can you increase your income ?
Which type of farming system do you advocate ?

Land Ceiling

Have you heard about land ceiling ? Yes No
Do you favour it ?
To whom should the land go ?
Have you lost/gained land due to ceiling ?
What should be the size of land holding ?

Use of Resources and Technology

Do you use your resources in an optimal manner ?
Do you get easily the services for your implements ?
Do you utilize your family labour fully ?
Do you utilize your draft-power fully?
Do you hire-out family labour, if yes,
how many days in a year ?
Do you exchange your family labour ?
(mendays in year)
Do you hire out your bullocks ?
Do you hire out your Tractor ?
(Hours in a year)
How do you thresh your wheat ?
Where do you take your sugarcane ?

Awareness

Have you heard about Five Year Plan ?

If yes, do you know the present plan period?

Do you know about C.D.Programme ?

Have some developmental plans brought change in village life ?

Do you know the location of your block ?

Do you read any newspaper ?

Do you listen to radio regularly ?

Attitudes	Yes	No
Do you know that the rate of population is quite high in India ?		
How would you control your family ?		
Do you favour family planning ?		
How many have adopted it in your family ?		
What should be the right age of marriage ?		
Reasons for non-adoption of F.P.		
What should be the number of children (boy and girl) a couple should have ?		
What type of family system do you prefer ?		

Caste System

Do you believe in caste system ?

If yes, why ?

Are you in favour of concessions given to Scheduled and Backward Castes ?

Do you invite Scheduled Caste persons to celebrate function ?

Do you favour inter-caste marriage ?

Institutions

Agency which have helped you ?
What do you feel about your Panchayat ?
Are the Cooperative Societies really useful ?
Have you rendered some help in village scheme ?

Habits

How many of your family members smoke and drink ?
Do you prepare tea daily ?
Do you prefer veiling system ?
Are you involved in some litigation ?
Do you think your standard of living not satisfactory ?
What is your source of entertainment ?

Politics

Do you know names of some political parties ?
Are you a member of some political party ?
What is your preference for Vote ?

Migration

No. of earning members migrated to other places.
No. of dependent members migrated to other place
Completely migrated to urban areas.
Do they take interest in village life ?
Level of remittance to family (Rs.)
Do you wish that your children follow your occupation ?
If not which occupation would you prefer for them ?
If given opportunity would you like to migrate to some city ?
Why, give reasons ?

APPENDIX—B

GLOSSARY OF THE LOCAL TERMS

Local terms	English equivalent and explanation
Ausoj	One of the desi months
Ayurvedic	Medical system based on Ayurveda
Babul	Acacia, twigs are used as tooth brush
Badha	Fixed land rent in terms of cash
Baithak	Drawing room exclusively for men
Bajra	A variety of millet ; the grain is made into flour
Balmiki	A sub-group of Scheduled Caste in the village who perform as sweepers and scavengers
Baniya	A vaish caste whose occupation is money-lending, shopkeeping or business
Banjar	Barren land
Barseem	A kind of important green fodder
Batai	System of share cropping
Bidi	A kind of smoke-stick made from tabacco rolled in a leaf
Bhadva	One of the desi months
Bhajan	A form of song mostly devotional
Buggi	A type of horse/mule/buffalo cart fitted with rubber tyres

Chamar	Leather worker and a sub-group of Scheduled Caste.
Charpay	Cot
Chaupal	A building used for public meetings in the village which also serves as a lodge for marriage-parties.
Chatni	Sauce
Chowkidar	Village night watchman who also serves as an attendant to the government officials that visit the village.
Chulha	A conventional stove used in open for cooking
Chunda	A traditional hair style adopted by village women almost now obsolete. It is a sort of 'Puff' where hair is collected and tied in the middle of the head.
Dai	Untrained midwife
Dal	Pulse
Dalia	Gruel
Dehati Programme	A Radio programme for the ruralities.
Desi	Local, traditional or indigenous
Falgun	A desi month (covering a part of the later half of March and early April).
Ganga	Name of most sacred river in India.
Gandli	A rope with coloured cotton threads mopped with peacock feathers and garlanded to the cattle on the eve of Divali.
Ghagra	A lower garment resembling petticoat but much heavier. It is fast getting out of fashion in the villages.

Ghee	Refined or clarified butter.
Ghewar	A kind of sweet prepared in the month of August (Sawan)
Gram Panchayat	A statutory body of elected representatives in the village.
Gram Sevak	Extension worker in the field of agriculture.
Gur	Jaggery
Halwa	Pudding
Harijan	It means people of God. This broad name was given to the untouchables by Mahatma Gandhi.
Hukka/Hookah	Tobacco pipe (also called a hubble-bubble) with a long flexible or fixed tube through which smoke is drawn through water in a vase and so cooled.
Jajman	A word of respectful intent used by a Scheduled Caste person to address an upper Caste person.
Jamuna	A sacred river next to the Ganges
Jantor	A kind of crop which yields green fodder and firewood.
Jowar	A summar crop which provides an edible grain and staple fodder.
Kharif	A blanket term used for summer crops
Khati	Carpenter
Khir	Sweet dish prepared by cooking rice in milk
Khichri	A light salt food preparation made by boiling rice and pulse together or millet and gram in combination.
Kohlu	Sugarcane crusher
Kothliwala bajra	Hybrid millet

Kucha	Any structure made of mud bricks.
Kumhar	Potter
Lambardar	Who collects land revenue and Chulha tax from the villagers.
Lassi	Butter milk
Lohar	Blacksmith
Masoor	A kind of lentil
Mator	Peas
Missi-roti	Bread made of wheat and gram flour
Mogra	A heavy stick used for washing clothes
Nai	Barber
Neem	A medicinal tree whose green twigs are used as tooth brush in the village.
Nirodh	A brand name for male contraceptive
Ojha	Sorcerer, a witch doctor.
Parda	A kind of veil
Parsad	Sweet-meat, fruit or any other eatable distributed by the person who observes fast, or after making an offering to some deities.
Patwari	Revenue official who maintains accounts of land and collects revenue in village.
Poli	Drawing room exclusively for males.
Pucca	Anything built with cement and concrete or brick and mortar
Puri	Wheat flour food item fried in ghee or oil.
Purnima	Day of full moon light
Rabri	Liquid salty food prepared from wheat, barley or bajra flour after slight fermentation.
Rakhi	A multicoloured decorative thread tied to the wrist of brother by his sister on the eve of Raksna Bandhan festival.

Rupee	The basic unit of currency in India.
Safeda	Eucalyptus
Sakar	Crystal sugar
Samlat	Common land
Sankh	Conch
Saradh	A fortnight in September when traditional rituals are observed for oblation to the dead in the family.
Sarson	Mustard (seed or plant)
Sawan	A desi month
Shiva	An important Hindu deity among highest trinity
Shivalya	Temple of Lord Shiva
Sindhara	A package of gift received by the newly-wed woman sent by her in-laws in the month of Sawan.
Singhara	A furit grown in pond or stationary water. It is rich in carbohydrate.
Sunar	Goldsmith
Subedar	Non-commissioned officer in the Indian army
Suhali	A sweetend wheat flour food item generally fried in mustard oil. It is prepared during Sawan (July).
Swang	Rural song and dance theatre where performers are all male. It is staged in village compound, street crossing or any other public place. The general tenor of performance is entertainment and didacticism.

BIBLIOGRAPHY

Ahmad, Jahir : *Dusk and Down in Village India*, Pall Mall Press Ltd. London, 1965

Bardan, P.K. : On the Incidence of Poverty in Rural India of the Sixties, *E.P.W.*, Annual Number, February, 1973.

Bhagat, A.S. : Resurvey of village Gijhi, Distt. Rohtak, Govt. of Punjab (Board of Economic Enquiry) 1960

Bhardwaj, Krishna : Tenurial Conditions and Mode of Exploitation : A Case Study of Some Villages in Orissa, 1975

Bhattacharya, J.P. : *Methodology of the Study of Rural Change in India.*

Bliss, C.J. and Stern, N.H. : *Palanpur : The Economy of an Indian Village*, Oxford University Press, Delhi, 1982

Board of Economic Enquiry : An Economic Survey of Nangal, Govt. of Punjab, Lahore, 1930

Dahiya, L.N. : Impact of Optimum Agricultural Land Allocation Patterns on Farm Incomes—A Case Study of Transitional Agricultural Economy, *IJAE*, Jan.—March, 1976

Dahiya, L.N. : Assets Distribution Among Rural Households, *Eastern Economist*, Feb. 12, 1981

Dahiya, L.N. and Jain, A.K. : High Yielding Variety Programme in Rohtak and Thanesar Blocks, *Journal of Haryana Studies*, Kurukshetra University, Vol. V, 1973.

Dantwala, M.L. : A Profile of Poverty and Unemployment in 12 Villages, *IJAE*, April-June 1975.

Darling, M.L. : *Wisdom and Waste in the Punjab Village*, Oxford University Press, London, 1934.

Indira, R.R. : Poverty, Inequality and Economic Growth in Rural Punjab 1960-61 to 1970-71, *Journal of Development Studies*, July, 1975.

Ishwaran : *Tradition and Economy in Village India*, Allied Publishers, Pvt. Ltd. Bombay, 1966.

John, P.V. and Gupta, L.C. : Comparative Study of Some Aspects of the Levels of Living in Two Villages, *IJAE*, Jan.-March, 1963.

Leaf, M.J. : The Green Revolution and Cultural Change in a Punjab Village, 1965-1978. *Economic Development and Cultural Change*, January, 1983.

Lewis, Oscar : *Village Life in Northern India*, University of Illinois, 1958.

Madan, G.R. : *Changing Pattern of Indian Villages*, S. Chand and Co. Delhi, 1959.

Marriot Mc Kim, : *Village India*, Chicago, 1955.

Max Weber : *Economy and Society* (eds. Roth and Wittch) Barkley, University of California Press, 1978.

Mckim, Marriott (ed), *Village India*, Asia Publishing House, Bombay, 1961.

Miller, D.B. : *Caste and Economic Development in a Haryana Village*, Ph. D thesis Australian National University, 1971

Misra, B. : Study of Levels of Living in a Village in Orissa, *IJAE*, Jan.-March, 1963.

Mukherjee, R.K. and Gupta, S.C. : *A Pilot Survey of Fourteen Villages in U.P. and Punjab*, Asia Publishing House, Bombay, 1959

Nair, Kusum : *Blossoms in the Dust*, London, 1961.

Nanavati : A Village in Gujarat, *IJAE*, April-June, 1961

Narain, R. and Narain, B : *Punjab Village Survey No. 2* (Gijhi Village in Rohtak District) Punjab Govt. Lahore, 1932.

N.S.S Report : Report on Indian Villages—Study of Some Social and Economic Aspects. Report No. 45

Neab, W. The Limitations of Indian Village Survey Data, *Journal of Asian Studies*, 1957.

Pande, V.P. : *The Origin, Development and Problems of Village Community Projection in India*, Ph. D thesis University of London, 1965.

Patel, R.M. : Some Issues of Rural Research and Development, *Arth Vikas*, Jan. 1985.

Pardhan, M.C. : *The Political System of Jats of Northern India*, Oxford University Press, 1966.

Randhawa, M.S. : *Green Revolution*, Vikas Publishing House, Delhi, 1979,

Shah, S.A. and Bedi, I.S. : Levels of Living in Rural Areas, *IJAE*, Jan-March, 1963.

Sharma, S.P. : Indian Village as a Unit of Study, *EPW*, Aug. 1969.

Smith, W. : *Modernization of a Traditional Village*, Asia Publishing House, Bombay, 1965.

Srinivas, M.N. : Village Studies Participant Observations and Social Research in India, *EPW*., Sept. 1975.

Talcott, P. : *The Social System*, London, Taristock Publications, 1952.

Verma, H.S. : *Post Independence Changes in Rural India : A Pilot Study of an U.p. Village*, 1980.

Vaswani, K.N. : Objects and Methods of Rural Surveys, *IJAE*, July-Dec. 1947.

Wiser, W.H. and Wiser, C.V. : *Beh'nd Mud Walls 1930-1960*, Barkeley, University of California Press, 1971.

INDEX